Ticket to Life

Embrace Uncertainty

A Journey to Emotional and Financial Freedom

November 2019

For Chris

By Erich Perroulaz

*Attidude is everything.
Keep focussed on
your own life dreams
Good to know you Erich*

Ticket to Life, Erich Perroulaz, Selfness & Wellness

Copyright © 2015 by Erich Perroulaz

Publisher: Selfness & Wellness(www.selfness-wellness.com)

SELFNESS & WELLNESS
L I F E   L O V E S   Y O U

All rights reserved. No part of this book may be reproduced or transmitted in any form without permission in writing from the publisher, except by a reviewer who may quote brief passages for review purposes.

First Edition

Introduction

"Don't be afraid; just believe, and she will be healed."

Luke 8:50, Jesus

A Message from the Author

I think it's important for all who will consider reading and using this book as a guide in their daily lives to know why I wrote this book and to know a little bit about me. Like many of you, I learned about something called the "Law of Attraction" through the popular 2006 film, "The Secret". If you aren't familiar with the film or The Law of Attraction, in its simplest form, it is the universal law that governs everything that comes into our lives, whether we want it to or not. The idea has often been claimed as esoteric, or "New Age". But this idea — or "law"— is the foundational principle of the history of the world. The Bible even presents the concept — though without a specific name — encouraging readers to think about things that are good, lovely, and true.

Understanding The Law of Attraction simply as the principle by which reality operates, we realize, too, that the most fantastic part about it is that it is something we can control and affect by changing the way we think. The law responds not only to our conscious and subconscious thoughts but also to our emotions. Those who can control their thoughts and mindsets can literally manifest whatever they want in life.

When I first learned about this idea, I thought it was a bit far-fetched, but I put what I had learned up to that point to work in my own life. I realized over time that the core of the ability to manifest what you want through the Law of Attraction comes down to one's ability to visualize, believe, and respond emotionally to draw in what you want to bring into his or her life.

Most people learn to visualize by simply "seeing what they want" in their heads, then imagining they already have it. However, I soon discovered that this method was not working for me. In fact, I couldn't visualize effectively and respond emotionally to something I couldn't actually see or hear.

I wanted to learn more about how other people made visualization techniques work for them. Accordingly, I began a journey that allowed me to consult self-help mentors, read books; eventually, I started to see my own life as a Law of Attraction experiment. I began absorbing stacks of course material, learning about scientific mind programming techniques such as NLP (Neuro Linguistic Programming) and ETF (Emotional Freedom Technique). I discovered subliminal messaging, and how it could be used to affect the subconscious mind.

Along the journey, I discovered a powerful mix of elements, which all together create a "super cocktail of mind-altering goodness". The secret to making it all work together is the awareness of a missing link, which I will cover in this book. I started to create a process manual that can change the lives of those who commit to applying the techniques and ideas the way I did.

I followed the step-by-step guidance in my own book as a self-experiment and wrote down the different "base camps" on the way to reach emotional and financial freedom. What happened after that was almost shocking. I actually started to feel safe and comfortable with myself without thinking about this journey. I could not believe it was true at first, and I was afraid to fall back into my old habits.

I continued to practice the techniques of the Law of Attraction daily, and like a dream come true; I continued to grow toward a new way of being. I found peace and the courage to focus on doing only what I actually loved and enjoyed doing. I can honestly say that this happiness came from a satisfaction with rediscovering who I was rather than where I was (or the exterior world). The Law of Attraction was finally on my side and visualization was working for me.

I knew I was onto something so I wanted to help as many people as I can. I wanted to teach them what I had discovered. I wanted them to solidify what they wanted in the same way that I did. So I decided to put my notes from the last 10 years into a book with the express purpose of guiding and inspiring readers to apply the Law of Attraction, start their own journeys toward self-understanding, and see their responsibility in a new and different perspective.

In addition, I wanted to share what I had learned with as many people as possible. I have received emails daily from people who have used my videos to change their lives. Receiving an email brings a satisfied smile to my face; the happiness is doubled knowing that I have helped someone achieve his or her dreams. That's why I created "Ticket to Life" and other brands like Essential Rich and Selfness & Wellness.

If you are ready to take the next step and accelerate towards your new life, then I encourage you to obtain your Ticket to Life. Time is precious, and my now constant state of emotional freedom and clarity was worth everything I owned. You will read later on just how my journey affected every aspect of my life. There is nothing to lose; in fact, there is, and a whole new world to be gained!

All I ask is that you take a few minutes of your time and consider what you want in life and its worth to you to be able to get there. This book is your guide in reading, practically executing pieces of advice offered in other books, and finally putting your own life into motion.

A Note to the Reader

All changes require effort and power to overcome internal resistance. Give yourself time and find people of similar mindset who can offer and likewise receive support. I remember arriving on the second day to the "Millionaire Mind" Training Seminar and noting that about a third of the people had not arrived. The trainer taught us that overcoming resistance and going for the next step, or the next day in this case, is always the key to achieving success. In short, the winners arrived for the next session. The losers preferred to stay in their comfort zones at home.

How to Read this Book

Why is it so difficult for most people to open their hearts to do what they really love doing? To guide you quickly towards learning and internalizing these powerful principles, I organized this book into three parts. Part I, "Preparation and Training," contains three chapters which outline the first stepping stones you must follow to get from where you are to where you want to be. You'll start by exploring the absolute necessity of taking 100% responsibility for your life and your results.

From that point, you'll learn how to clarify your life's purpose, your vision, and your passion. This journey does not have shortcuts. It's not about getting to the destination; it's about undergoing the process completely.

Olympic athletes, top entrepreneurs, and world leaders all undergo preparation and training in order to end up victorious. We'll look at how to create an unshakable belief in yourself and your dreams. I'll then help you transform your vision into a set of concrete goals and an action plan for achieving them. I will also talk about how I was able to harness the incredible power of affirmation and visualization—one of the secrets to success for all.

Part II, "Standstill, Endurance and Healing", talks about the phases in the process that can make you uncomfortable sometimes. To address this concern, I will share action steps that are needed to make your dreams come true. You'll learn to ask for what you want, rethink rejection, solicit and respond to feedback, and persevere in the face of what can sometimes seem like insurmountable obstacles. Part II also addresses the important inner work you'll need to do, which will help you remove any mental and emotional blocks that might be impeding your success. However, it's not enough to know what to do, as there are many books that will tell you that.

Therefore, you also need to understand the importance of, and the methodology for, removing self-defeating beliefs, fears, and habits that are holding you back. These blocks can significantly slow your progress; it's like driving your car with the emergency brake on.

Part III, "Move Forward without Looking Back", highlights the last stages in this journey. In these chapters, you will learn powerful principles that will change the way you view the world. These are important steps that you may have overlooked in the past. The ability to accomplish these steps often separates the successful from the mediocre people in life.

My wish for you, my friends and dear readers, is for you to allow me to guide you in this journey, on a path that I've personally been on. It will be my joy to mentor you through this book. Feel free to take what you need and leave out what you don't agree to. Nevertheless, I encourage you to receive this book with an open mind and an open heart. Give it a chance. Take it as an experiment like I did. Truly, your life will never be the same again. If you're looking for a full life, then buy your Ticket to Life.

Dedication

For all humans out there who starve for inner peace and want to achieve a higher level of consciousness, and feel the power of love.

Be winners, renew your attitude, never quit learning and growing, and transform all unhealthy and low energies into a higher vibration called abundance.

Table of Contents

Introduction		v
	A Message from the Author	v
	A Note to the Reader	viii
	How to Read this Book	viii
Dedication		xi
Table of Contents		xiii
List of Figures		xx
Prologue	The Illusion of the Monetary System	xxi
	A Crash Course in the Current Monetary System	xxi
	The Federal Reserve System	xxii
	When Paper Replaced Gold and Silver	xxiii
	Emotional Millionaire	xxv
Part I: Preparation and Training		1
Chapter 1	Where It All Began	5
	Crossroads	5
	Reaching the Epitome of Success	6
	Still Stuck	7
	Only You Can Direct Your Subconscious Mind	8
	The Law of Attraction	10
	Growing the Dream	10
	Crash and Burn	12
	Fake ID	13
	"Being" is the True Path to "Having"	13
	The Road to Canada	15

	MENTOR'S SECTION: WALLACE WATTLES	17
Chapter 2	Hitting the Dead End	18
	The Rat Race	18
	Hiding behind a Mask	20
	The Blame Game	22
	Rethinking You or Me	23
	Operating from the Do-Have-Be Mindset	25
	The Language of the LOA	26
	Overcoming the Dog-Eat-Dog World	27
	The Tip of the Iceberg	28
	The Slave Mindset	29
	Survival	30
	The Beggar and The Slave	30
	Setting Holistic Goals	32
	Defining Your Feelings	33
	Transforming Your Blueprint	34
	MENTOR'S SECTION: DR. JOSEPHY MURPHY	36
Chapter 3	Discovering Your Blueprint	37
	The Key to Emotional Freedom	37
	The Power of Emotions	38
	Your Own Brand	38
	The Company of You	39
	Overwriting Your Blueprint	40
	The Life of Illusion	41
	The Master Plan	42
	The Process of Discovery	43
	Aiming for Clarity	45
	Going Against the Ego	45
	Poor Blueprint vs. Wealthy Blueprint	47
	Setting Your Emotional Mindset	48
	Give Your Emotions a Concrete Name	48
	Emotional Upgrade	50
	Preparing for Showdowns	53
	Taking Control of the Moment	53
	Don't Worry, Be Happy	54

	How I Received Confidence to Depart for Canada	55
	How I Received a Rent-Free Home	56
	Don't Let Uncertainty Hold You Back	58
	Embracing Uncertainty	58
	Letting Go of Past Limitations	59
	Elephants and Us	60
	I'd Rather Be Rich Than Right	60
	MENTOR'S SECTION: T. HARV EKER	62
Chapter 4	The Universal Laws of Success	64
	The Power of the Media	64
	Water is Water	65
	Coming from a Place of Abundance	66
	The LOA and Your Blueprint	67
	Getting Out of the Rat Race	67
	The Product of Worry and Fear	68
	The Value of a Master Plan and Life Script	69
	Making the Shift	70
	Waiting Game	73
	Be Able to Delay Gratification	73
	Shifting from Victim to Master	73
	When Thoughts Become Reality	75
	MENTOR'S SECTION: RHONDA BYRNE	76
Part II: Stand Still, Endurance, & Healing		77
Chapter 5	Look in the Mirror	81
	The Man in the Mirror	81
	Facing the Music	81
	The Cost of Living Life Unexamined	82
	Curing Burnouts	83
	Getting off the Rollercoaster	84
	The Freedom of Self-Awareness	84
	Breaking Free	85
	The Universal Law of Identity	86
	The Link between Integrity and Workability	87

Table of Contents

	Embracing vulnerability	87
	The Illusion of the Mask	88
	Giving up the Reins	89
	Taking an Honest Look	90
	Touched by an Angel	90
	Archangel Michael	91
	Fasten Your Seatbelt	92
	MENTOR'S SECTION: PAOLO COELHO	94
Chapter 6	Follow Your Joy	95
	What makes you happy?	95
	Emptying Yourself Out	96
	What Makes You Truly Happy?	97
	Detachment	98
	All-In	99
	The Power of 1%	100
	Be the Author of Your Joy	102
	Happiness without a Reason	102
	Position of Entitlement vs. Position of Gratitude	103
	Playing Small	103
	Playing Big	104
	Be a Farmer	105
	Sowing and Reaping	105
	The Law of Deliberate Creation	106
	Operate in Faith	106
	Develop Patience	108
	What Season Are You In?	108
	The Butterfly Experience	111
	Before you can dive, you need to learn to swim	112
	Learning the Ropes	112
	Facing the Facts	113
	Dwelling on Joy	114
	MENTOR'S SECTION: DR. JUDITH ORLOFF	115
	MENTOR'S SECTION: ASTRONAUT EDGAR MITCHELL	116

Chapter 7	Forgive the Past	118
	The need to cut ties	118
	Shifting Gears	119
	Journey to my roots	120
	Forgiving my roots	121
	Reconnecting	121
	Open your heart	122
	Forgiveness frees us from limiting beliefs	123
	The Life Sentence	124
	Reversing the Life Sentence	125
	Healing	126
	Three Emotional States	126
	First State: Wearing the Mask to Please Others	126
	Second State: Waiting for Somebody Else's Help	126
	Third State: Moving Forward Without Fear	127
	How a Life-Guide Can Help	127
	Leadership and Forgiveness	128
	The Sick Monetary System	129
	Breaking the Ties That Bind	131
	MENTOR'S SECTION: ELIZABETH CLARE PROPHET	132
	HEALER'S SECTION: MARGRIT BERISH	133
Part III: Move Forward Without Looking Back		135
	Feelings, Emotions, and Market Prices	136
Chapter 8	Practice Gratitude Now	139
	The Power of Humility	139
	The Law of Vibration	141
	The Space for Gratitude	142
	Embedding Gratitude into your Blueprint	143
	The Situation has Nothing to do with your Gratitude	144
	Grumbling vs. Gratitude	145
	Gratitude and the LOA	146
	Steps to Living in Gratitude Today	146

Table of Contents

	Emotion-Based Goal-Setting	147
	MENTOR'S SECTION: MARIE FORLEO	149
Chapter 9	Live with Abundance	150
	A Life of Abundance	150
	A Posture to Receive	151
	Serendipity	152
	The Fear of Lack is the Denial of Vulnerability	155
	Breakdowns are a Blessing	156
	Gaining Leverage	158
	The Essence of Love	159
	The Power of Connection	160
	Speak out Loud	161
	Courage to Stand Up	162
	Life is a Contact Sport	163
	Get your Audience	164
	Believing in Abundance Leads to Emotional Freedom	165
	Symptoms of a New Blueprint	166
	Sealing a New Blueprint	167
	MENTOR'S SECTION: STEVEN SPIELBERG	169
Chapter 10	Let it Happen	171
	The Gourage to Let Go	171
	The Bank of Life	172
	The Law of Allowing	174
	The Tent and the Rain	175
	Let it Come in Its Own Way	176
	What you Resist will Persist	176
	Your Life Mailbox	177
	Play Big	179
	MENTOR'S SECTION: JORDAN BELFORT	180
Chapter 11	Meet your Future Self	181
	Why Professional Athletes have Coaches	181
	Pointing out Blind Spots	182

	A Growing Field	183
	The Life Entrepreneur Academy	185
	Essential Matching in Relationships and Life	185
	Mentors Took me Through the Journey	186
	You Attract What you Focus On	187
	Steps to Having a Life Guide	188
	Be a Contribution	190
	MENTOR'S SECTION: SIR JOHN TEMPLETON	191
	MENTOR'S SECTION: TOM HANSBERGER	193
Special Chapter	Wealth Without a Job	195
	Why are Rich People Wealthy?	195
	Being Essentially Rich	196
	Attachment to Money vs. Attachment to Purpose	197
	Success vs. Mediocrity	198
	180-Degree Change	198
	Emotional Freedom is the Key to Financial Freedom	200
	The Birth of a New Monetary System	201
	The Phases of a 180-Degree Transformation	202
	MENTOR'S SECTION: ROBERT KIYOSAKI	203
Epilogue	The Journey to Angel Mountain (Engelberg), Switzerland	205
	Preparation and Training	207
	Stand Still, Endure and Heal	210
	Moving Forward without Looking Back	218
Bibliography		223
An Invitation to Come Visit Angelmountain (Engelberg)		227
Acknowledgements		229

List of Figures

Figure 1: Leave the Drama Zone	24
Figure 2: Gatekeeper	47
Figure 3: Emotional Bondage Thought Process	51
Figure 4: Emotional Freedom Thought Process	52
Figure 5: The Router of Confidence	70
Figure 6: Emotional Condition Barometer	72
Figure 7: Attitude for Wealth	99
Figure 8: Performance Road Map	107
Figure 9 Life Zone Model	154
Figure 10: Crossing the Finish Line	168
Figure 11: Money Tree	174
Figure 12: Change Focus	200
Figure 13: The Journey of Emotional Transformation	206

Prologue
The Illusion of the Monetary System

> "I believe that banking institutions are more dangerous to our liberties than standing armies."
>
> – Thomas Jefferson

A Crash Course in the Current Monetary System

It is unfortunate, but understandable, that people in the United States and all over the world are not taught (most especially in government's schools) the history and the operation of their country's most powerful financial institution, the central banks. Among all of them, the leading central bank of the world always dominates the world reserve currency.

Today, the U.S. Dollar is still the most influential currency, and so we like to put some light on the central bank of the United States, called The Federal Reserve System FED. Created in 1910 and codified by Congress in 1913, this "system" facilitated the U.S. government's ability to inflame the nation's citizens to support the European war of 1914-1918 (World War I).

Several of these same Wall Street banks financed Adolf Hitler two decades later. My experience in the investment business gave me a sense of satisfaction and the opportunity to learn about trading and investment banking. But despite those pluses, I had a strange feeling about what money really

Prologue — **THE ILLUSION OF THE MONETARY SYSTEM**

is about and how it was connected for human's personal development. Have you had similar feelings? It felt strange that I earned my money in a system, which was not clear to me.

This book is not about the inner workings of the monetary system, so I will not go into further details about it. However, I suggest that you do your own research to understand who really is in the seat of power of world politics and what effect this has on your daily life. I was shocked when I discovered the secret and what this had to do with my blueprint and habits.

The Federal Reserve System

The system of central banks uses the paper monetary system to gain power over people. Despite what many economists and I have learned about how to control monetary policies, inflation and deflation, central banks still have the control. The paper monetary system was used in ancient times; for example, it was used to finance the Roman Empire or to keep the French Kingdoms afloat. In more present history, in 1910, a group of powerful men that time met secretly on an island off the coast of Georgia, on Jekyll Island, to create a privately-owned and powerful entity. It was called the Federal Reserve System.

Just in case you desire to know more about the international interests and subsequent political relationships of the bankers who created the Federal Reserve System, I recommend the book, "The Creature from Jekyll Island: A Second Look at the Federal Reserve Paperback" by G. Edward Griffin. Reading said book would definitely change your worldview. You'll never trust a politician again—or a banker:

> "Where does money come from? Where does it go? Who makes it? The money magicians' secrets are unveiled. We get a close look at their mirrors and smoke

machines, their pulleys, cogs, and wheels that create the grand illusion called money. A dry and boring subject? Just wait! You'll be hooked in five minutes. Reads like a detective story - which it really is. But it's all true. This book is about the most blatant scam of all history. It's all here: the cause of wars, boom-bust cycles, inflation, depression, and prosperity."

On the Christmas Eve 1913, the U.S. Congress passed the Federal Reserve Act, which officially gave the power to private bankers (the Federal Reserve Corporation) to create money, and away from the United States congress. Take note, these are private bankers. You might not have realized it but such occurrence is very influential in your own life, especially when you live in a western country.

A few years after signing the 1913 Federal Reserve Act, U.S. President Woodrow Wilson wrote:

> "I am a most unhappy man. I have unwittingly ruined my country. A great industrial nation is controlled by its system of credit. Our system of credit is concentrated. The growth of the nation, therefore, and all our activities are in the hands of a few men. We have come to be one of the worst ruled, one of the most completely controlled and dominated Governments in the civilized world no longer a Government by free opinion, no longer a Government by conviction and the vote of the majority, but a Government by the opinion and duress of a small group of dominant men."

When Paper Replaced Gold and Silver

In the U.S. and in a lot of other countries around the world, people are living in the age of fiat money. The U.S. dollar has no intrinsic value. This paper money currency is no longer backed by gold or silver, but it is the recognized and required currency by the federal government as legal tender. In fact, no assets back money; money is backed by debt.

THE ILLUSION OF THE MONETARY SYSTEM

Money is debt and it is only valuable for trading purposes for as long as people still have faith in their governments. Is there an alternative out of this system trap? I say yes, and that's one of the key reasons why I wrote this book, through which you will need to see your self-esteem as your main currency in life as it always were.

Paper money has no intrinsic value. Why do you have to work hard to achieve a piece of paper with no real value? I know this is a controversial question since we all live in this system. You work hard and exchange your life power into something, which loses buying power every day. Welcome to the hamster wheel!

What can you do to secure your assets from the paper money buying power devaluation? Well, you can choose to have self-responsibility and do your own research. I leave it up to you if you want to leave your money on a bank account, or if you want to take some cash out of the system and invest it on real assets like precious metals and stocks of companies.

What about investing your money on real estate? Well, as long as it provides free cash flow for you and it's an asset, then go for it. However, for most people, real estate is a liability. Remember, as long as central bankers print money the interest rates will stay very low and provide you with the illusion to stay in this system forever. The prices of real estate can go up or down so fast. It's almost unbelievable how people haven't discovered this monetary illusion and how more people have been led into it.

Physical ownership of precious metals can give you security in "changing times". These precious metals, like gold and silver, have kept their value over 2000 years. Some people call their precious metals "real money" since these precious metals need a working process until a silver coin or bullion is manifested. The process is similar to a person's emotional journey to achieve the physical manifestations he desires through the Law of Attraction, as we'll see later in the book.

Whenever the government is in need of money, it borrows from the Federal Reserve, which, as I mentioned earlier, isn't a government institution, but a cartel of private banks, created by powerful banking family names in Jekyll Island in 1910 and established by Congress in 1913. This Fed "creates" the money the government needs in the form of government bonds, ultimately made out of "paper and ink". The government then spends this money, which ends up as deposits in private bank accounts, where it is used in turn to back up private loans. More money is created "out of nothing" since banks typically lend $9 for each dollar they have in deposit! As you can see, all money is created out of debt. If all debts would be paid, then all money would literally disappear. Therefore, paper money, which is not backed up by gold, is an illusionary monetary system.

I strongly suggest that teachers in all public schools be courageous enough to educate themselves about money and entrepreneurship to give their pupils and students the real choice in their lives. Will the next year be a total US financial collapse, a stock market crash or a massive inflation? Frankly, I don't care! Because my fate does not depend on the economy (and yours shouldn't either). How about investing in something that's real and something that's genuinely priceless?

Emotional Millionaire

How you can become an "emotional millionaire"? This book talks about the missing link that you've been looking for in this paper-money-driven world. Society has created a gap in you that you've continuously filled with material wealth, with the hopes of becoming emotionally stable and satisfied.

THE ILLUSION OF THE MONETARY SYSTEM

This book takes you on a step-by-step guide to emotional freedom, which ultimately leads to financial freedom. You'll see this to be true because this is how the Law of Attraction works. Your emotional status dictates the reality of your experience. Allow me to be your life guide as you take on this journey with me. Allow me, too, to mentor you to operate with the blueprint of an emotional millionaire. Because once you become an emotional millionaire, you'll never be bankrupt—ever.

Part I
Preparation and Training

If you believe in a materialistic worldview, you may need to take a second look at what really makes life go round. You may be adhering to an illusion. Your feelings are guided by your thoughts and inner pictures, so if you believe that you need more money, status, and recognition in order to feel better, it may be worthwhile for you to shift gears and change your way of thinking—now. Yes, money is important, but it might come to you from a different order of command.

By order of command, I mean the way you think about things, and the way you have always thought life should go. Most people go to work to make money and then hope that inner well-being follows. Why won't you change this order to first get well within yourself, then work out of this center and let the money come to you?

I just want to give you an idea of what I did in the last 10 years. Well, I changed the order of command for myself—and it worked. Why do parents, teachers and other authority figures in our lives not teach this order of command to our children? Well, if this order of command were taught to them, the world would surely change. If you can recall, the dominating worldview 500 years ago claimed that the earth was flat and that it was the center of the universe.

People like Copernicus provided a different order of things and shook the worldview that people held so dearly. He observed that something did not quite add up. He was not content with the worldview that was fed to him from childhood. Eventually, he searched for a better explanation for why the world was the way it was believed to be it was. Could it be the same today? Could we potentially revolutionize the future by learning and teaching a new way of viewing and doing life?

During this same period, Johannes Gutenberg invented printing techniques for books and papers. His invention opened the door of accessibility to ideas and truth for the common man. This was the Renaissance period, which was immediately followed by a period of Reformation. People like Leonardo da Vinci, Albrecht Dürer, Dante Alighieri, Niccolo Machiavelli, Erasmus, and William Shakespeare began to reveal their brilliance during this time. It was a period that truly changed worldviews.

Just a few decades old, the Internet marks another invention of an information medium, which gives people the freedom to research ideas that were previously far removed from them, such as those about economics, philosophy, politics, and life-changing principles like the Law of Attraction (LOA). Books like "The Secret" by Rhonda Byrne provide a way to present the techniques and principles of positive thinking, the power of feelings, and of using the LOA to experience a life of freedom.

With periods of change occurring every few hundred years, I believe that we are in another period of transformational worldviews. Why is it still so difficult for people to really enjoy a life of emotional and financial freedom? I believe that the reason is that the old order of command of DO-HAVE-BE is still taught in schools and by authority figures whom we have always looked up to. They are the ones who ultimately will benefit from this kind of system. So give the new order of command, the BE-DO-HAVE, a chance.

Chapter 1
Where It All Began

> Whatever results you're getting, be they rich or poor, good or bad, positive or negative, always remember that your outer world is simply a reflection of your inner world. If things aren't going well in your outer life, it's because things aren't going well in your inner life. It's that simple.
>
> - T. Harv Eker

Crossroads

I looked at the time. It was very early in the morning, but I was already stressed. I had to get to work by 8 a.m. I headed out the door, making note of the other people who were also on their way to work, and I saw nothing but blank stares—a reflection of myself looking back at me. Were they all feeling what I was feeling?

Day in, day out, this was my life. I woke up early to go to work, and then hustled my way through the day, putting on a successful and unfazed front. But deep inside, I felt tired, weak, and miserable. I realized that this was not the life I wanted to live.

During that time, I was working at an investment boutique. By the world's standards, I was living a successful life. The lifestyle I was exposed to and the environment I was in was fast-paced. I was a young professional on my way to the top of my career.

But there I was, commuting to work and dreading the thought that this would be how every day of my life would look, sound, and feel.

My mind drifted back to my childhood, to a time sitting in the car with my mother. As we listened to the radio I asked my mom what the announcer was speaking about. She told me he was relaying the quote updates for the day's stock exchange. She explained the idea of stock exchange in a simplified way. At that early age, I became enamored with the idea of trading and envisioned myself working as a trader. True to the law of which I yet knew nothing, this vision became my reality early on in my career.

Reaching the Epitome of Success

Growing up in Switzerland, I was surrounded by a culture in which one was defined by success and wealth. One had power if one had a job that brought in a lot of money. This was what I wanted for my life, even as a child.

I started out as an intern in the Business Bank Commercial School. This impressed girls. This impressed my mother. This impressed a lot of people. Most of all, it impressed me. During that time, I thought that I had it all together. I thought *this was my road to happiness*. I was so sure that when I finished my internship and became a trader, I would be satisfied. I was quite pleased with myself because I felt that happiness and success were about attaining everything that culture had told me I wanted —a nice job, a luxury car, a huge condo, and people looking up to me.

Little by little, I started to realize that the bubble I lived in was an illusion. But I tried to push aside whatever inklings I had that it was not the life I wanted, because it did not make sense to me. *Why wouldn't I want a life with a prestigious career and the opportunities to be rich and powerful in society?* It was crazy talk. So I locked up the little voice in my head into a metaphorical drawer that I thought I'd never revisit.

Working in financial institutions in Zurich and Geneva, I was grateful to be there, as I knew that only a few people are given this opportunity. The bosses I had saw my potential as a trader; they challenged me to continue improving professionally. Yet, the mundane, day-to-day life I had in the office drove me to seek change. Every day, everything was the same. The culture in the workplace was structured in such a way that there were minimal relationships formed, especially if you did not join in any post-work activities.

I was *in* the social scene, but the relationships I had were superficial. We were together for parties and post-work drinking sessions, but that was all it was. There were no true friendships formed. There was only a surface-level connection. The fact that I thought I was *in* the social scene was an illusion in itself.

At that time, I didn't really see the real *me*. I thought the antidote to whatever it was that did not sit well with me was simply a change of scenery. So, I literally placed myself in a different place. I moved to the U.S. the moment a career opportunity opened up. I left to be a Wall Street guy—and I impressed myself.

Still Stuck

As a child, I dreamt of working in the U.S. But when I arrived in Atlanta, GA, it was as if I had just built an entirely new prison for myself. No matter where I was, in Switzerland or in the U.S., I had this feeling that I was stuck; I was miserable. I found myself trapped again; it was just that this time I was in a different country. Regardless of where I was, emotionally I was still in the same place of "stuck-ness".

I worked in the U.S. for one long, desperate year. I was like a mouse caught in a trap. My bosses drove me crazy; they worked me like a milk cow because they made a commission on top of my commission. Because of the time difference in Europe they wanted me to be in the office as early as 4 a.m. I had thought this was the life I wanted. I had wanted to live and work in the U.S. to escape the life I had in Switzerland when I was dreading each day I had to go to work. But when I got there, I realized that I was still unhappy. What was missing?

Looking back, I realized that what I was experiencing was not only happening to me. Negativity is a human trait that projects itself within our consciousness too often. Somehow, whatever we do, whatever we have, whatever image we project, we are still prone to remaining in a chaotic and confused state on the inside. It seems that too many of us find ourselves locked away behind our own self-made prison walls.

We ask ourselves, *why can't we be free*? But have we tried asking ourselves, *who holds the key*? We remain trapped initially because we pretend to be okay. We think, *this is just the way life is*, or, *I have no right to complain; I have everything I need*. Why can't we be honest about the void that we feel within? As Werner Erhard puts it, we need to be "authentic about our 'inauthenticity'."

Only You Can Direct Your Subconscious Mind

Even if we don't admit it aloud, our pretensions to being okay do not change the questions and confusion that exist in our minds behind the happy smile. There is some degree of unhappiness that exists in our subconscious. The scientific phenomenon of self-fulfilling prophecy is always at work under the term of the LOA. Whatever we think will come back to us manifesting in positive or negative ways based on our mindset. Our thoughts and the behaviors that follow them set us up for either success or failure.

Our subconscious mind responds to the mental pictures we have inside. The subconscious mind takes its "marching orders" from the pictures and images we allow inside, and then silently creates the conditions that we feel, believe, and think about.

We might say that we desire all the good things in life, such as health, happiness, peace of mind, and abundance, but a number of us have spent their lives frustrated over the fact that they cannot achieve the results they want for their lives.

When deep inside we're miserable, confused, and discontent, we attract misery, confusion, and discontentment. Have you noticed that chaos and misfortune have become cycles in your own life? In my case, I noticed that the more I attempted to ignore the misery and discontent in my spirit, the more it appeared as my reality. There's a misalignment that generally exists within us; in fact, most of us are not able to mentally or emotionally unite with the good we desire to see in our lives.

This book is not about new perceptions or new ideas. I wrote this book to serve as a practical step-by-step guide to applying the little-known but longstanding Law of Attraction for your benefit and to obtaining peace from the chaos. My life has been a depiction of how this law works—and it does work whether you like it or not, whether you're aware of it or not, whether you honor it or not, and whether you believe it or not.

The Law of Attraction

> **TRANSFORMATION PRINCIPLE 1:**
>
> *The LOA functions like an order and delivery system in which you can "order" the universe to deliver what you want through your subconscious mind.*

The Law of Attraction (LOA) is an energetic vibration that bounces back the energy you send out, much like a boomerang. It matches the emotions and thoughts you dwell upon by creating a manifestation of these things in your conditions and circumstances. The LOA functions like an order and delivery system in which you can "order" the universe to deliver what you want through your subconscious mind.

The LOA is always at work. Whatever energy you send out to the world—when it becomes powerful enough—will be recreated on a physical level. Every human being vibrates on an energy level, which manifests his or her real life experiences. I've seen this law at work in my own lifetime, and time again, even when I didn't know it had a name.

Growing the Dream

From the young boy who was instantly interested in trading from the first time he heard about it on the radio, to the bank intern, to the actual trader, I had become an entrepreneur. Yet even so, something in me was searching for something beyond the confines of the four walls of my office. There was something missing despite the success that I had attained as a trader. Because I didn't want to be a slave to my bosses anymore, I thought that I should manage my own business. I eventually started my own company thinking that maybe it was what I had been looking for all along—freedom from the corporate world. Maybe it was what would finally make me feel happy and complete.

During this time, I was privileged to meet a great man and investor by the name of Tom Hansberger. He was a former partner of the legendary Sir John Templeton and ran his own asset management company. I instantly felt that this connection could change everything. And it did. I opened up an investment sales and marketing business.

My goal was to match the value investment style with a fund company in Switzerland to receive ongoing income by growing the assets. I began to understand that sales and marketing are some of the most important assets of an entrepreneur. At this time I was hustling around town telling my story and introducing the asset management style to investors and fund companies in Europe. It worked.

Finally, I launched my business with two investment funds that had enough assets to continue growing. My business was successful. During this time, I traded my account. One morning my broker told me that the net worth was bulging in the high millions. It may sound like a huge success story. But this was, in fact, the beginning of my downward spiral.

I was supposed to be on top of the world. I had my own company. I had money in the bank. Yet no one knew about all these successes. They knew my business was picking up. But they did not know that the stock market had already made me a millionaire.

I was living in fear. It was an odd feeling to get what I thought I had always wanted, but after obtaining it, realized that my fears and limiting beliefs were actually robbing me of the experience of enjoying the fruit of success.

Crash and Burn

At that time, I never told anybody that I had made millions. Deep inside, I was fearful. I feared a lot of things. Everything was chaotic for me. Since I had made my money in the stock market, I was constantly checking up on my stocks. This was before the age of smart phones and Wi-Fi, so it literally consumed my time. Even when I was at lunch with others, my mind was adrift. It wandered aimlessly back and forth, wondering what was happening with my money at that moment. I was neither mentally nor emotionally present in my life. The stock market's fluctuations took control of me, putting me in a constant state of discontent and need for more and more to feel I had reached my dream.

I made millions of dollars, but never understood a single thing about how and why the stock market actually moved. I had been a fool of coincidences because all of that happened during the Internet bubble and I was not the only one to strike it rich during that time. I thought I needed to acquire more, but that need came from a place of desperation rather than peace and abundance. My subconscious mind picked up on that.

The subconscious mind always picks up on your strongest emotions. During that time, the strongest emotions I was feeling were fear and desperation. I had no knowledge about the Law of Attraction. The thing about laws is that they will be true to themselves and carry out whether or not one is aware of them. As quickly as my success had come, it dissipated. The stock market bubble burst, and all my money was gone.

To add insult to injury, the market trouble forced the closure of my company, even while we were in the process of hiring new people. I was in shock; it felt like I had caused this somehow.

I was seeing a psychiatrist and he was giving me medication to help me recover from depression. But the medication didn't help; it just calmed me for the moment. I'm aware now that my depression was not due to a loss, but to the devastation of realizing that I didn't know who I was. And because I didn't know who I was, I was also unable to address what I actually wanted out of life.

Fake ID

Have you ever driven with a fake driver's license? When you are eventually caught, your car would likely be confiscated and impounded. Until that point, you live in fear of being caught, and that's a terrible way to live. In my whole life, I pretended to be someone who I thought I *should* be. What about you? Who are you pretending to be?

We often allow external things to dictate our identities. The clothes we wear, the cars we drive, the gadgets we have, and the houses we live in measure who we are. Sometimes, we're dictated by the kind of work we have or the kind of people we have relationships with.

If you don't proactively set your own identity, it will simply be a reaction to your circumstances, possessions, and relationships. You will take on an identity that has been placed upon you by life, or by other people. Ultimately, this doesn't work. It doesn't work because it isn't authentic. It doesn't work because it's not the true expression of who you are.

"Being" is the True Path to "Having"

When I lost all the money I had worked hard for, it was like a physical manifestation of what I was feeling inside – lost. There was a complete disconnection between what I was doing and feeling and who I really was. I've realized since that period in my life that I was only playing the part of a successful trader. In reality, it was not who I was. Don't get me wrong: trading is still one of my favorite things to do today. I really enjoy it. But it is not and never has been the core of me.

Most of the time, we're trapped in the concept of "having" without understanding our core *being*. Society teaches us to do things in order to have things in order to reach our goals and be someone we want to be. Furthermore, society also dictates that we have to work hard to have the best things in life. When we have the best things in life, then and only then can we be happy or feel significant in this world. That might be true, but for those who feel dejected, that won't work that way. Most people are left empty, disappointed, frustrated, and depressed because after all the efforts to accomplish something and acquire the things they had thought they needed, the feelings of insignificance remain.

We need to realize that nature dictates action. A fish swims because it's a fish. The nature of a fish is to swim. The *being* of a fish includes the action of swimming. If you know how to swim, does that make you a fish? No. Acting like a fish by mimicking its actions doesn't make you a fish—even if you swim 24 hours a day, seven days a week. You'll never be a fish, because this is not your nature.

When you discover your true "being", you can act according to your nature. When you act authentically, you can have the freedom that you innately need as a human being. Each of us has a unique "being", a blueprint that depicts the way we're designed.

In order to align your actions, behaviors, and desires with your identity, it's imperative to understand who you are. One of the reasons why we experience internal chaos and confusion is that we all have valid needs, which we are not able to meet due to a lack of awareness of who we really are.

WHERE IT ALL BEGAN · Preparation

When I look back at the things I had and did, I realize that those did not reflect my true nature. While I had wealth and worked as a trader, I knew that something was not right. But I didn't have the courage to face myself and to admit this. I didn't want to admit that my life was not good enough. When you look at your own life, do you also struggle to recognize that there is something missing and that it has been missing for a lot longer than you'd care to admit?

The Road to Canada

I made a decision for myself that day. It was the best decision I had ever made in my life because it led to the turning point that brought me to where I am today. After three years of being paralyzed in my condominium undergoing mental therapy that never really helped, I decided to step out of my comfort zone. I decided to leave Switzerland for Canada.

The infamous "comfort zone" is your status quo. It's the way it has always been for you—the comfortable, safe way of life. When you stay in your comfort zone, you don't do anything new or anything that could possibly expose you to uncertainty. Going back to my story, I stepped out of the security and certainty; I stepped *outside* my comfort zone.

The transformation of my life began when I recognized that I needed to discover my true *being*. I remember telling myself, "You're not coming back, until you know the answer to the question: 'Who are you?'" How many times have you felt that whatever is going on in your life does not coincide with what you desire or what you've always expected? It is so easy to blame it on circumstances. The realization I had was that I needed to have the courage to question my life. I needed to discover if what I was doing aligned with the purpose my life was intended to fulfill. Moreover, I wasn't quite sure what that purpose was just yet. When you look at your own life, what do you think is missing?

When I look back to the times when I was at my lowest, I'm able to pinpoint the lack of emotional freedom in myself. I used to just sweep my emotions under the rug in order to function and survive. I was living on survival mode on the inside, while on the outside it seemed like I had everything I needed to live a full life.

My subconscious mind sensed the internal struggles and manifested themselves in the loss of my millions and my company. Could I blame the economy? Sure. I could blame every person, thing, and situation I wanted to blame. But it wouldn't get me anywhere.

My decision to go to Canada marked the first time I actually took responsibility for myself. It was a giant leap of faith—it was *my* leap. It was not something anyone dictated for me to do. It was not because I wanted to impress anyone. It was something I had to do for myself, to *find* myself.

That was the time of reckoning. But the journey from Canada to the present was the real adventure: it was the journey to myself, and can also be the journey to *yourself*. The next chapters will guide you in reaching your own emotional freedom. The financial wealth will come if you follow every step of the process. Some chapters may seem repetitive, but you should read them anyway because every reading provides new insights and realizations.

In conclusion about this chapter, the road from Canada to Angel Mountain in Switzerland (where I now live) is my personal experience of the ultimate life experience and how the Law of Attraction works beyond theory and in reality to uncover the missing links and misguidance that people encounter regularly in their daily lives.

MENTOR'S SECTION: WALLACE WATTLES

It's been a hundred years since Wattles published "The Science of Getting Rich", but its legacy lives on to touch lives of millions of people, including mine. Marked by humble beginnings, Wattle started his childhood in a farm in Illinois with his parents. His father was a gardener and his mother a housekeeper. With little formal education, Wattles worked as a farm laborer and travelled to Chicago and studied the writings of Ralph Waldo Emerson and the teachings of Jesus. Going beyond scholarship, he went ahead to put these great men's theories into practice and experienced success and wealth in his own life.

Known to the people closest to him as a pragmatist, Wattles lived every page he wrote in his book and challenged his readers to do the same. Wattles' example is something close to my heart, because as I was writing this book, I simply recalled the experiences and lessons I learned while taking on the journey to emotional freedom.

Wattles' life teaches us that wealth doesn't come from being graduates of the best schools or from being members of rich families; instead, it's from thinking and acting in a certain way. It is in our mind, our thoughts that hold the key to our prosperity. Our thoughts bring us closer to what we want. Many of those who succeed with their thinking have failed to translate these thoughts into actions, thereby ultimately preventing them from experiencing what they desire. It is through your actions, your life performance that you can attract what you want to you.

> **There is an abundance of opportunity for the man who will go with the tide instead of trying to swim against it.**
>
> **- Wallace Wattles**

Chapter 2
Hitting the Dead End

> "There is no such thing as a hopeless situation. Every single circumstance of your life can change!"
>
> — Rhonda Byrne, "The Secret"

The Rat Race

Every day, millions of people around the world are caught in a competitive and self-defeating cycle of trying to attain wealth. This cycle is accurately termed, 'the rat race', conjuring images of a lab rat running helplessly to and fro in a maze, never able to get out and win. The only way you can ever hope to escape the rat race is to dive deep into your belief system. It's neither simple nor without implications, because it will certainly affect your personal image of life.

To escape the maze that you may quickly find yourself in, you must question your current reality as taught to you. Without questioning your reality, you will likely have the desire to take shortcuts to change. The first thing you need to realize is the true blueprint of the world we live in. The original design of the world was for it to work for <u>you and me</u>. However, society teaches us to operate under a different set of rules. We have been taught to live and to survive in a world that works for you *or* me. Why not accept a blueprint of "as well as" instead of "either" or "instead"? Do you see the difference?

HITTING THE DEAD END

If you play according to the rules of the world that works for "you *or* me", you'll operate in terms of survival and selfishness. The reason why we experience life as a rat race is that we've been living in a world using the wrong set of rules and principles. When you're going against the natural design of the world, you're bound to experience resistance and limitations. But why is this set of rules so strongly anchored in most people's minds?

Have you ever tried driving with an utter disregard for traffic signs? You would never continue to move forward if the sign said, "One Way" or "Dead End" unless you intentionally wanted to crash your car; otherwise, you would turn your vehicle around and find a different route. However, in their own lives, people move forward despite the signs that warn them against doing so. They don't necessarily want to harm themselves; they just don't know any better. The conflict begins because they see the world through a different lens and apply a different set of rules that cause them to disregard the signs before them.

Unfortunately, *ignorance* of the true law excuses no one. Even if you do not know the laws that operate beneath the surface and within the subconscious mind, you are still bound by them. This is how the rat race is sustained. The fact that people operate under a set of rules different from those of the *real* reality keeps them running in a rat race, preventing them from getting anywhere no matter how hard they try.

Instead of operating by the true law, people look to temporary solutions. The world that works for you *or* me is run by monetary wealth. The one with the most money is the one with the most power, and the one with the most power is the one with the most money. But nobody can win this game because there will always be somebody with more assets or power around. Yet nobody will recognize or admit it until that moment when they are forced into a situation that no amount of power or money can resolve. By then, they will be forced to come face to face with the true nature of the universe. Only then can they see the true blueprint of life and realize that they've been stuck in a rat race.

Living your life as a victim of circumstance means you let external people, conditions, and things dictate your emotional well-being. The start of a vacation is filled with euphoria. But the end is met with the dread of going back to the daily grind. Going back to my past, when the stock market was rising, I was happy. But when it tanked, I felt the misery of it all. Accordingly, it's exhausting to be controlled by external things, and frustrating to have no control over your emotions.

No doubt you have faced situations like this, in which you felt helpless, and that no amount of money would ever help you find a way out. Perhaps you have felt stuck, and wondered, *"Is this really how life will be for me until I die?"*

Hiding behind a Mask

In my life, I've worn many masks. I was wearing a mask when I worked for companies for the sake of money rather than for the well-being of my customers.

When we wear masks we are simply behaving in the way that we think other people want us to behave. In most cases, we think this is the best way. However, we often disregard the fact that acting in such an inauthentic way will have long-term consequences for our lives.

While I recognized the disconnection between my feelings about the job requirements and what I actually wanted in my life, I went through my day wearing the mask that told everyone that I was exactly where I wanted to be. But that couldn't be any further from what I was truly feeling.

Being overworked or facing a conflict of interest with your boss can put you in situations where you must decide about remaining true to your feelings on the matter, or in doing what your boss expects you to do. I experienced this many times, but I had to keep closing the deals.

During those times, I was wearing the mask of the nice guy who was happy with his life. No one could tell I was feeling intense emotional pain inside. People never want to know about your issues and problems. They want to hear that all is well rather than the authentic fact of the situation.

People feel they *have* to wear masks because they are in denial of their true nature, hence afraid to be found out. In addition, they're afraid to reveal who they really are because this world dictates a mold for how and who you're supposed to be. They're afraid that the world will discover their insecurities, imperfections, and shortcomings.

In the world that works for you or me, you must maintain a slave mindset because doing so means that you're serving a purpose--you're standing in line, you're following orders.

A major part of society believes in visible or measurable wealth rather than the unlimited abundance and creation that the inner world can create. When you understand how the blueprint works and what your real purpose in life is, there won't be any need to wear a mask. Only then will you ever understand that being authentic has infinitely more power than wearing a mask.

People wear masks to belong to professional networks or family systems, to land better jobs, or to develop relationships. They simply want to fit in. However, when the goal is to fit in, you will ultimately experience only an illusion of what life could be. And when you're operating from a mask, you deceive yourself about being someone who you're not.

When you are inauthentic in whom you are conflicts are bound to arise. Your subconscious mind will detect your lack of authenticity. It will detect that you are hiding the fears, the anxiety, and the insecurity. The subconscious can do so because it is not a fool; it can see beyond the masks and cause the feelings that lie behind the smile to become your reality.

The Blame Game

One of the most devastating times in my life was when I moved to an apartment just to be near a woman I thought I was in love with. The day I moved, she told me that she did not want to see me anymore. My heart was broken. Money could not address what I was feeling. I found myself stuck in a place I did not belong and I no longer had a connection to.

Oftentimes, we give another person the power to rule our lives, our emotions, and our decisions. We do this not because of sacrificial love, but because we simply don't want to take responsibility for being in charge of our own happiness.

When we assign the responsibility to other people, things, or to anything other than ourselves, we mistakenly think doing so will give us a "get out of jail" card when things do not go our way. We think that in doing so, we won't end up getting blamed. But again, this is an illusion we create for ourselves. You and I cannot disregard the fact that we must be responsible for our lives.

A circumstance in my life revealed to me that people in the world operate in a "you or me" world, where there's always a winner and a loser. In any scenario, you want to be the winner. But operating under these rules means that in order to be the winner, you should make someone else the loser.

I decided rationally to move forward without fear and to act despite tremendous doubts. During this time, I moved back to my home region with a new attitude to make another attempt at my life. From the outside I appeared to be a loser; but on the inside I had already made a quantum leap that shifted my experiences from being a slave of emotions created by other people or circumstances to being a master of my own destiny. I began to realize that there is a state of mind, which can be called "consistent inner freedom" or "emotional freedom".

In the past, my feelings, decisions, and behavior were all dictated by circumstances. As a slave of circumstance, I knew that I did not have the power to make changes in my life. At the same time, I didn't have to take the blame for being enslaved by circumstance. I did not have to be responsible for how things turned out. I simply went with the flow.

Rethinking You *or* Me

Now, with no girlfriend, no place to stay, and what seemed like no dignity, I gathered myself up and went back to my old home. I learned a tough lesson that I should never move for a job or a relationship. That decision had not been based on a "you *or* me" world perspective; it *was* based on making life-changing decisions based on circumstance or temporary emotions. I had simply been trying to fill a void within myself, which, I thought things, status, or people could fill. But the answer couldn't come from the exterior. It had to come from within me.

When I moved to the U.S. for a job offer, I realized that I had always been operating as a victim of circumstance. My motivation for acquiring money or success came from a non-supportive root of fear, anger, or the need to prove myself in society. However, money never brought me any happiness, inner peace or even freedom. In a world that works for you *or* me, success is defined by the education, intelligence, skills, work, contacts, or luck you have. It's always a competition. Success roots from the desire to be better than the next person. Real success results from living a life that's authentic to your blueprint.

Many of us have areas in life that we refuse to accept responsibility. Think about your life for a moment. How many times have you allowed people or circumstances to dictate your life decisions? In playing the blame game, no one really wins. The person, or thing, whom you've assigned blame to, will not win because, at least in your perspective, he or she will be responsible for your pain and suffering. You won't win either, because you have turned yourself into a victim of circumstance rather than the master of your life.

LEAVE THE DRAMA ZONE

LIFE PERFORMER

VICTIM

Low Energy Field

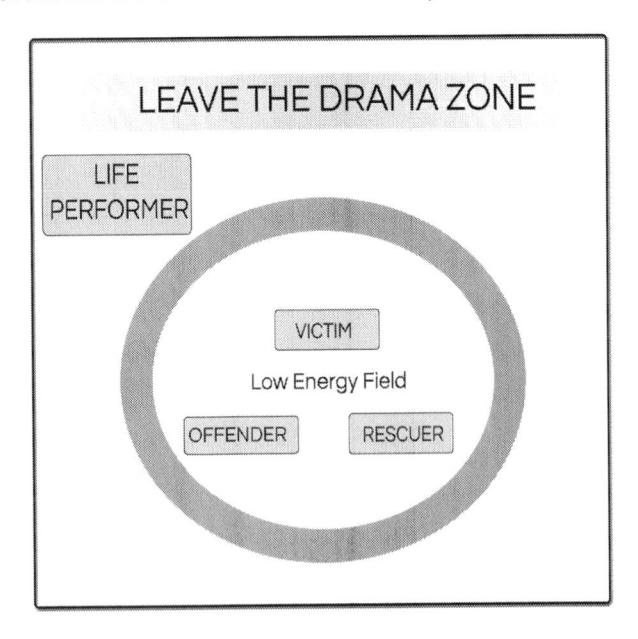

OFFENDER   RESCUER

Figure 1: Leave the Drama Zone

When functioning in the low-energy field of the rat race, the only roles you'll get to play are limited to being the victim, the offender, and the rescuer. However, when you step out of your comfort zone into a high-energy field, you'll get to be the life performer. This is where you should strive to be. Leave all the drama that exists in the low-energy zone and achieve emotional freedom so that you can truly perform in your life.

Operating from the Do-Have-Be Mindset

> **TRANSFORMATION PRINCIPLE 2:**
>
> *If you are living in the moment in what is known as 'the now', then you just ARE. In this condition, you are aware of your own purpose of life and act from your core.*

What is the Do-Have-Be Mindset and how can you change that mindset to Be-Do-Have? If you are living in the moment in what is known as 'the now', then you just ARE. In this condition, you are aware of your own purpose in life and act from your core.

You do things because they make you happy and just because they give you joy; there's no need to focus on what you can get, because living your life like this places you in a position to receive positive things. By practicing delayed gratification, you will receive much greater, long-term rewards. This is called the Be-Do-Have order.

Most people live in a problem-solving world, in which they simply react to problems as they face them. By shifting to the Do-Have-Be order, you will continue your life in the rat race because you are part of the system. Work, work, work, or income might collapse.

There is an income far greater than the monetary—it is the income that is realized at the harvest of your purpose in life. So when you operate from a defensive mode to solve a problem, you can't take the time to reflect and to consider how these decisions will impact the big picture. You simply react in the established way within the established system.

The key to getting out of the rat race is found in transforming your blueprint. Instead of trying to cope in a problem-solving world, you need to operate from a blueprint in which you are the author of your life. You create your life. You create your circumstances.

People who live in a problem-solving world focus on the problem. And so, when they look at a glass, they see it as half-empty instead of half-full. Their habits are based on a negative and problem-oriented view. Whenever these people try to do something extraordinary or life changing, they instantly think about what could go wrong. In their minds, they already assume that any leap of faith they take is bound to be doomed. From this perspective, people won't give themselves a fighting chance to be successful. So, my advice to you is that you have to be honest with yourself about your own tendencies toward this.

The Language of the LOA

A person's language reveals the mindset by which he or she is operating. Unfortunately, the power of a negative person's language is also self-destructive. A person who has a problem-solving mindset would say something like, "I hope it doesn't rain today" or "I hope I don't lose money." Instead of saying, "You're welcome," a negative-minded person would say, "No problem." This person often uses *negative* words in his sentences. This is a recipe for manifesting a life of failure and negativity.

The Law of Attraction (LOA) does not understand negations. According to this law, you are simply inviting the manifestation of "rain", "losing money," and "problems". If you operate in a problem-solving mindset, you are probably unaware that your language can create your future. As a result, you will react emotionally to whatever happens to you. You will think that this is just how life is. Perhaps you'll believe, "Maybe I'm just not good enough" or "Maybe I'm just unlucky in life." And the cycle under this mindset will continue.

If you understand that you can author your life based on the powerful thoughts you feed your subconscious mind and through the powerful language you speak, you will not be surprised when the things you desire actually manifest in your life. Remember, you need to <u>be</u> in order to truly <u>have</u>. But when you're stuck in this "you or me" worldview, you then start <u>doing</u> in order to <u>have</u>, in order for you to <u>be</u>.

Overcoming the Dog-Eat-Dog World

In this dog-eat-dog world, people work hard to have wealth, so that they can view themselves as significant. In the process of working hard, some people don't mind stepping on others or dragging them down. This is something that they <u>do</u>, in order to <u>have</u> success and power. When they <u>have</u> it, they think that they'll <u>be</u> significant in the world, and they will <u>be</u> content.

Sometimes people think that in order to *be* happy, they need to behave and do certain things and have certain things. They think that if only they had better relationships, more money, more time, or better health, they would be happy. But they never get out of the cycle of doing, having, and being. The worldview of the Do-Have-Be is the recipe for a sad, frustrating, and depressing life. You can never get from Point A to B by doing things in this way, because it is all backwards.

The blueprint for happiness and success must be established before anyone can truly be happy and bear the fruits of a content life. It actually starts from within, from the awareness of who you are and who you are *being*.

When you operate from the Do-Have-Be principle, your blueprint (being-ness) is dependent on your doing and your having. When your *being* is based on your performance, stress and pressure follow you daily. Questions such as "What if I'm not good enough?" and "What if I'm not strong enough?"

begin to emerge; you will have the natural tendency to operate in fear and insecurity.

When you operate in fear and insecurity, your subconscious mind will pick up on it and manifest it as your reality. Since your mind is constantly creating the conditions you feel and think about, running the rat race brings your worst fears in life.

The Tip of the Iceberg

When you operate from a mindset of fear, you will tend to focus on what you cannot change. But when you dwell on what you don't have and what you can't do, you give up yourself and give those thoughts the power to define you.

The problem roots from trying to change superficial things, like behaviors or approaches, as well as the criteria we use for decision-making. However, those problems are only the tip of the iceberg. Lasting change only comes by addressing the issues below the surface.

Imagine an iceberg and you're on your way to comprehending the idea of the blueprint. About 80% of your identity lies below the water line. Only 20% of your blueprint is exposed through your actions, behaviors, and decisions. The part that's hidden from the world is the part that's most powerful; it's your subconscious. It is made up of your skill set, your belief system, your values, and your "I am" statements.

When there are issues with any of those, problems will manifest in your language, actions, and goals. When there's an inner void, you cannot fill it with external things. You cannot keep looking for external things to make you happy. When you continue in this way, you're guaranteed to experience satisfaction, but only until the next time you're unhappy and looking for new things to fill you again. And the rat race continues.

Those who are stuck in the rat race always choose immediate gratification over long-term rewards. They lack patience to wait for something better, and are oriented to simply consume per the rules of the world that operating for you or me. They just take and take because they think that it's the only way to survive.

The Slave Mindset

I used to play the role of a slave in the social system—most people do. This may not sound nice (and it actually isn't), but it's easily accepted because this slavery provides the benefit of structural and materialistic security in exchange for freedom.

Inner freedom is marked by the ability to reach inner peace. Only genuine emotional freedom can lead to abundance and wealth. I took the journey, and I found that freedom as I learned what it meant to obtain my ticket to life.

In ancient times, society was made up of masters and slaves. The slave served the master. The master controlled the slave. The master dictated whatever the slave must do. The slave's complete obedience was required in exchange for food and shelter. The slave had a structure to his life that was predictable and, ironically, "safe". He didn't need to worry about what he would eat or where he would live because his master took care of it all.

But at what expense does your worrying cost? Freedom. The slave was willing to live a life of bondage so that he could survive. Survival was not about thriving. It was merely an act of existing. In the movie *12 Years a Slave*, Solomon Northup, an educated, free black man, was sold into slavery. He was told to hide his education and to pretend to be dumb to survive. To this, Solomon replied, "I don't want to survive. I want to live!"

Prior to the realization of your true blueprint vs. you mask, you live as a slave. Maybe this is the mindset by which you're still operating right now. Maybe you're settling for a structured, predictable life even though it goes against your true identity.

Survival

The slave is easily satisfied. He barely has enough, but it's enough to survive. However, the slave is limited and powerless. Unbeknownst to themselves, many choose to live with a slave mindset because with freedom comes responsibility, and with responsibility comes the need to take off the mask, be real, and lead others toward the same realness.

More often than not, people fear responsibility. They also fear the uncertainty that lies ahead if they decide to leave the slave mindset. When you take a step out of your comfort zone and leave the mind of the slave for a new way of thinking and doing, the journey of transition will be a challenge, but it is one challenge that is well worth it. When slaves leave their old lives behind, they have nothing but their freedom. When you have nothing, what must you do? You need to beg. A beggar is better than a slave because a beggar is free. In his own way he is the master of his destiny. He may not have much right now, but his situation is temporary. Because he is free, he has the power to create new possibilities that he was not allowed as a slave.

The Beggar and The Slave

Oftentimes people look down on beggars because the latter have no money and are sometimes thought to be lazy. But remember, they are free, and with freedom comes a real future. In his book, Donald Trump talks about one of the hardest times in his life; it was when he was $900 million in debt. He was walking along the street and when he saw a beggar, he thought to himself, *if that man had nothing then* *he is richer than me by $900 million, because at least he had no debt.* But even when falling to this state, Trump did not allow his financial situation to dictate his way of being. He did not have the mindset of a slave. He had the mindset of a leader. And he was able to gain back all the money he had lost and become wealthy once again. He was a rich man on the inside.

Emotionally empty people, or what I call "emotionally bankrupt people," work hard to just earn money in hopes that doing so will fix all their problems. Trump is a prime example of how emotionally wealthy people experience setbacks; they don't remain in that state forever. Eventually, they always find a way to repair the situation, and when relevant, gain their wealth back but only by achieving emotional freedom and harvesting the results that follow. At the end of the day, your financial worth may go up and down, but your inner freedom and stability will last forever. This journey can be the adventure of your life. Are you ready to let go and to live?

One of the biggest reasons why people never make the shift from being a slave to being a beggar is that they're afraid to face the humiliation. They are afraid to ask for favors and to declare what they want. But it is when you are in this median place of transition that you can discover the humility that must be present as you move from 'having as a slave', to "having as a beggar" to 'having as a leader''; during such times you will be most open to realizing and accepting the good that comes your way. The humility of being in a place of need and want puts you in a place of gratitude rather than taking advantage of things and remaining unhappy. Instead of being frustrated, stressed, and concerned about everything that is missing in your life, let gratefulness and appreciation exude from your heart and mind.

When you overcome the fear of humiliation and when you are able to operate humbly, you will see your true power. You will find what it takes to operate as a leader rather than a follower. As a leader, there's no limit to what you can create and accomplish. A leader does not let other people dictate what he wants to do with his life. He knows who he is and he operates from the blueprint that *he* decides to operate from.

Setting Holistic Goals

A lot of us know what we want to achieve in life, but only a few of us know what we actually want to feel in our lives. But being able to define what we want in life is the key to freedom and wealth. People tirelessly chase high-paying jobs, attractive people, beautiful houses, and trips around the world. And for what are these? They ultimately *hope* to *feel* comfort, *feel* powerful, *feel* beautiful, you *feel* loved and significant. But they are disappointed every time, because the feeling will never last unless they change their mindset and invite good to manifest in their lives.

Are you setting goals for the best outcomes in your life? Or, are you setting goals to feed your Ego? Are your goals designed to impress others to support the masks you are wearing? I challenge you to make your goal the intentional discovery and revelation of the real you.

The idea of setting goals is not new. We're familiar with this, especially in the area of improving performance and achieving a successful life. However, listing your goals is often the easiest part. The key—the hardest part—is ensuring that somehow you are not overlooking the real goals that you truly want to achieve.

Most people get caught up in the goals that other people set for them. These pre-created goals play like a script in their heads that they're just following. They want nice houses, nice cars, around-the-world trips, wealth, and so much more. While these are good goals to have, the question is: *Why pursue these goals?* With that question is another point: *What purpose do they have in your life?* When you can't connect your goals to the real purpose of your life, your life itself will be meaningless even when you're able to achieve them.

When you look at life and decide to stop wearing your masks, you are taking responsibility for your life and deciding what you actually want to feel. The truth is that people wear masks because they also want to feel something. They're afraid that without their masks they won't be whom they want to be, or, rather, who have told (or dictated) that they need to be. You must be aware of these emotions. These feelings will be the elemental point on which your actions and your goal setting system will be based.

Defining Your Feelings

Because feelings are magnetic, they are automatically recorded in the subconscious mind. Being so, they have the power to manifest in your reality. Gratitude begets gratefulness. Love attracts love. Generosity produces a generous response. When your feelings are mostly focused on frustration, jealousy, and desperation, this is what you will manifest in your circumstances and conditions. To counter this situation, you must focus on the good things. At the end of the day, the only way you'll experience these good feelings is when you decide that you want to be free, powerful, and filled with new possibilities.

Decide for yourself how you want to feel about your career, your relationships, your health, and your wealth. If you have goals, write down the feelings you associate with them. Grab a dictionary and look up a definition for each of the words that describe your feelings. Enter into your emotional epicenter and imagine that you've already attained your desired lifestyle. Don't allow your desires to deviate from your real purpose in life. You can transform your wants into actualities once you understand that what you're looking for is already within yourself. When you focus on the internal rather than the external, you'll be able to connect with your authentic self.

Transforming Your Blueprint

Focusing on the inside means mastering the inner game of wealth. Through constant repetition of supporting affirmations and visualization of your own desired life's master plan, you can begin to overwrite the subconscious mind. Constant repetitions will create a shift in your feelings, which may only last awhile, so they will require self-discipline to maintain. You can bring about a renovation of the blueprint you want to have. Claim the feeling that goes with that envisioned blueprint.

It's like changing the course on a cruise ship. As the ship starts to move very slowly towards your desired life goals, you need to constantly focus on where you're going. Constant repetition speeds up the process of changing the blueprint. You need to commit to holistically transforming your blueprint each day. Sometimes, all it takes is about 10-15 minutes, twice a day, of entering into the mindset of the feelings you want to have.

After you wake up and before you sleep, focus on what you want to feel in your life. Focus on how you can bring these feelings into reality. Define the things you want in your life—are these about love? Significance? Nothing is too great or small to list.

To tap into the subconscious mind, also called the alpha condition, make it a habit to affirm the feelings you want to have. The last thing you want to do is take your emotional health for granted. Most of the day, you operate in your beta condition that helps you function logically. But you must intentionally bypass it and tap into the power of your subconscious mind. When you override the slave mindset you were operating in, you'll be able to see actual results in the conditions and circumstances you'll be facing.

MENTOR'S SECTION:
DR. JOSEPHY MURPHY

The book *The Power of Your Subconscious Mind* by Dr. Joseph Murphy was the first I've read about emotional freedom and inner power. By writing this book, Dr. Murphy did not seek to be famous or to satisfy his Ego; he simply wanted to share his philosophy with the world.

Dr. Murphy was born into a strict Catholic family of highly educated parents in the South of Ireland. He was raised in a world of books and entered the seminary to study for priesthood. When he completed his studies, he was ordained a Roman Catholic priest (although his life as a priest was short-lived). During the same time, he studied chemistry and earned his diploma as a pharmacist.

He worked as a pharmacist in New York where he met Abdullah, a well-known Ethiopian rabbi and professor. Through Abdullah, Dr. Murphy learned the power of the subconscious mind, the *kabbalah* (an esoteric school of thought that originated in Judaism), the hidden meanings of the Bible, and the power of God.

Dr. Murphy's teachings reveal why some people are sad while others are happy, why others are poor and miserable and others are joyous and prosperous, why others are fearful and anxious, while others are full of faith and confidence. In his book, Dr. Murphy points out to the workings of our conscious and subconscious mind to determine the kind of life we'll live.

> **The Law of Attraction attracts to you everything you need, according to the nature of your thought life. Your environment and financial conditions are the perfect reflection of your habitual thinking. Thought rules the world.**
>
> **- Dr. Joseph Murphy**

Chapter 3
Discovering Your Blueprint

"Be happy for no reason, like a child. If you are happy for a reason, you're in trouble, because that reason can be taken from you."

— Deepak Chopra

The Key to Emotional Freedom

Before we dive into how you can discover your blueprint, you need to grasp the concept of emotional freedom. Most people are simply victims of their circumstances; they allow themselves to be enslaved by their emotions, to be people in bondage. Far too often, they simply don't know that they can be free, to begin with.

Emotional freedom occurs when your feelings are no longer dependent on your everyday circumstances. When you live in emotional freedom, happiness becomes a normal and constant state. In this state, you simply *are*. Nothing in you is dependent upon anything outside of you.

Emotions are the only driver for your everyday actions. If you're not aware about your actual blueprint, your actions will be based on your circumstances. Your emotions will be based on external things rather than internal factors. This will allow other people to control and manipulate your emotions without trying.

The Power of Emotions

We experience emotional manipulations every day. Take a look at all the ads that surround you. Everywhere we look, there's an advertisement, which makes you *feel* something that will cause you to *buy* the product that the ad is promoting. Why do companies spend millions of dollars for advertising spots and to build their brands? That is because they know the science of emotions and feelings. They also know how to implant an idea in your mind that demands a response.

Brands evoke emotions. Think about your favorite brands. Coca-Cola isn't a Christmas product, but the commercials and image that they've created over the years tend to evoke holiday warmth and cheer, which are good feelings that you want to continue. Nike's *Just Do It* brand can motivate you toward a more active lifestyle. Apparently, these companies understand that once you're emotionally sealed with the brand, they will forevermore be able to connect with you on a subconscious level. When people's emotions are captured in this way, they almost always choose the product they feel they are connected with.

Your Own Brand

A brand of a product or service represents a company to the world. This representation is the character by which the world knows a company, along with its products and services. A brand embodies the core values of a company.

In looking at your own life, what "character" do you see yourself portraying to the world? Is it authentic and does it reflect who you really are? Or is it a mask behind which nobody has ever seen?

People quickly label others based on emotions that they associate them with, and nobody wants to be around a downer unless he or she is a downer himself or herself. Do you inspire or motivate those around you, or do you tend to tear them down? People feel burdened by the presence of too many negative emotions. It's time to evaluate the vibe you are sending out to the world—if it's negative, stop! What emotions are evoked when you think about yourself? What emotions do you feel when you think about your personal brand? You need to ask these questions so you will know if you like the brand message you're sending out about your life to the world. Think about the level of satisfaction you have about your brand. Is it a source of distress and frustration for you?

Do you know that you can actually create your own brand? When it comes to building the brand of a company, marketing experts start from the inside out. Internal branding must take place before any external form of brand building can begin. For a brand to be sustainable, it must be integrated into all activities within the company. To do this successfully, a company must make sure that the values that the brand represents need to be authentic and organic, which is a natural *way of being*. For example, if a company's brand is its customer-centric approach and high-quality products, then every system within the company should be based on these values. Whether it is the sales department or the manufacturing team, the processes and purposes of the work of the people under either department should be directed toward delivering high-quality products and making the customer the center of their processes.

The Company of You

If you imagine yourself as a company, what would your brand be? Would it be a successful, emotionally and financially free person? Or is it the one you *want* to portray, though deep down you feel that something isn't connected? The thing about brands is that consumers know when it's a hard sell. A hard sell is when a marketing strategy is used that's too aggressive through the use of forceful language. Customers can smell if something is inauthentic. Are you portraying a brand that is true to your true *being*?

Analogously speaking, core values are to a company while your personal blueprint is to you (your true *being*). Just as a company's values influence its strategies and activities, your blueprint determines your behavior and your way of thinking. The vision of the company serves as the map that the company follows to know where it will go in the future; it's the indicator that it's getting somewhere. But your master plan, not your blueprint, should be the gauge of your success: that is, the amount of money in your bank, the number of friends you have across the spectrum of social media, or the sharp intellect you claim to possess should never be considered as bases to measure your success or happiness. Instead, the true measure of your success is determined by how close you are to fulfilling your purpose here on earth.

It's never too late to renovate the false blueprint of self-destruction in which you've been living. You can overwrite and change it to align it with your real desires in life. Understanding your blueprint will explain why you do what you do. If your blueprint is made up of limiting beliefs, then behavior and actions will reflect the limitations.

Overwriting Your Blueprint

What do I mean by "overwriting your blueprint"? How is this done? First, you need to understand how your blueprint is formed. Your blueprint is the source of your current life situation; however, your current blueprint is changeable! The secret of successful people is that they are aware that they need to constantly improve and expand their blueprint in order to get powerful results in the future.

Your blueprint contains the power of the subconscious mind. Your experiences dictate your way of thinking, and your way of thinking dictates your current blueprint in what can become a cruel cycle if not directed properly. For example, you can direct your subconscious mind to have joy that transcends all understanding, and then you will start experiencing happiness that is not dependent on any external thing.

Most people operate using the blueprint of the world. When you operate from a blueprint that you yourself did not author, then you're just a character in your story rather than its author. If you are not conscious of being a slave to circumstance, then you will not be able to detect your blueprint. You will not be able to recognize truly what you want in your life because you will see the world from a lens that it is *what it is*, and you have no power to change it.

The Life of Illusion

We humans tend to accept illusion as reality. But once we begin to realize that we are living in denial as slaves wearing masks to fit in, and then we can start releasing ourselves from this rat race.

I came to that point, and stood face-to-face with the fact that I was operating from a blueprint that someone else wrote for me. My blueprint was that of trying to make money and trying to find my place in the world.

However, at the base of all the things I tried to do and accomplish, I was afraid that if I didn't <u>do</u>, people would see me as a loser. Fear, anxiety, and desperation were my constant friends. Of course, these are not the friends anyone should spend time with.

The mind must be in control of the emotions so you will be able to overwrite your blueprint. But oftentimes, our non-supportive emotions take control of our mind. However, once you have identified these emotions that cause you to behave against yourself, then you have taken one positive step toward change.

Have you ever been afraid? When you're afraid your mind creates a situation that you believe will happen, even when it may never materialize. This places you in a state of fear. If you imagine fear as the illusion that it is, you will come to see the futility of this negative emotion. You tremble in vain at an imagined scenario of *what could* happen, but it's not really happening.

The process of overwriting your blueprint will allow you to get rid of unwanted feelings buried in your subconscious mind. This process must be viewed as a preparation. A chef will say, "mise en place"? This means you need to line up the ingredients in their proper places before you can start cooking.

Returning the example of company branding, the core values of the company need to align with the vision of the company. Every action a company takes should reflect its brand. In the same way, your *way of being*, which refers to the totality of your behaviors, your actions, your decisions, your language, and your thoughts represents your blueprint and should, therefore, be aligned to define the real you.

The Master Plan

The master plan represents your true purpose in life. It is what makes sense of your *being*. It is what you're here to accomplish. Anything you do on earth that brings you closer to fulfilling this purpose will always bring you a higher level of joy and satisfaction. When you pursue something that doesn't align with your master plan, you may find yourself in a state of temporary happiness, only to find that something is still missing. If you're honest with yourself, you'll admit that you've noticed that something has always been missing.

It doesn't matter if you have the most sought-after job in the world. It doesn't matter if you have millions in the bank. It doesn't matter if society regards you as wealthy and successful. It doesn't matter where you travel. If you're going against your master plan, you will end up feeling frustrated, disappointed, and incomplete. I know this truth because I have lived it.

A clue as to what your master plan is can be seen when you're doing something that gives you joy. When you're doing something not just because you need to pay the bills but because you enjoy it, you are following the right course for your life. It's the dream job you may have had, but you had set it aside because you thought people might think it was silly or impossible to accomplish.

Each one of us was created in such a way that at some point we would gravitate toward our purpose. This is how we were designed. Until we realize our master plan, we will always feel a longing and an emptiness for something that we can't quite explain.

The Process of Discovery

Where do you see yourself five years from now? Before you answer hastily, paint a picture in your mind of where you want to be in your life in a world without limitations. For this exercise, make sure to allot the amount of time that you think changing your life deserves. Listen to your inner voice. Only you are responsible for figuring out your purpose in life. And you owe that to yourself.

For some, this exercise may not be easy because they have been operating in a world filled with limitations for so long that they can't move without considering the barriers they have to face. Nevertheless, whether it's a walk in the park or a bitter medicine to swallow, this is an important part of your journey. You need to be able to picture what you were placed on this earth to accomplish. Where and whom do you really want to be?

Imagine yourself again as the author of your life, and create your character sketch. What kind of life are you living? What kind of person are you? What are your values? What are your beliefs about life?

The more specific you can be, the better this thought experiment would work to give you clarity of the things that are important to you. Imagine yourself waking up in the morning. Where would you wake up? What kind of room would you have? Think about whom you would wake up to. Imagine whom you would have breakfast with. What kind of breakfast would you have? Would you be eating breakfast with your family? Picture your daily routine. Do you have a spouse and kids? If you want a spouse, imagine what he or she would be like. Picture the kind of relationship you would have with your family.

Imagine the kind of clothes you would wear. Where would you go after eating breakfast? Are you driving or walking? Determine what car you would want to drive.

Would you be headed to the office? What kind of work would you do? Decide if you are a professional at something or if you run your own company. If you have your own business, what kind of business it would be? Picture the kind of partners you would have. What kind of success would you have at this point? Picture yourself enjoying a hobby. What kind of hobby would it be? Identify what you would be doing for fun.

DISCOVERING YOUR BLUEPRINT — Preparation

> **TRANSFORMATION PRINCIPLE 3:**
>
> **Your life script will serve as a lighthouse on your journey. It will serve as a guide for where you will go in life.**

Aiming for Clarity

Your life script might be a bit fuzzy at this point. It takes time to build a life script and really know what you want. In my case, it took me quite awhile to really recognize and agree within myself upon my master plan. Anything that's important takes time. However, once you have decided to discover your master plan and have set the intention to author your life script, you will see things clearly.

Your life script will serve as a lighthouse on your journey. It will serve as a guide for where you will go in life. Set aside time every morning or evening to build on your life script. Invest the time to make this script more concrete so that you can build a vivid picture in your mind as to where you are headed.

To overwrite a destructive blueprint successfully, you need to get rid of every belief that doesn't support your life script. This is not easy, but it's not impossible. And it will be totally worth it.

Going Against the Ego

Before you can reclaim your real blueprint, you will have to disengage your Ego. The Ego plays the role of the guard. The Ego wants to keep the status quo. It wants you to go with the flow and remain a slave to circumstances because it likes security and stagnancy.

In order to overwrite your blueprint, you must find a way to overcome the guard in your head. You need to come from a place of confidence, not from a place of desperation. You can't think, *Oh no, I need to make this happen*. You need to come from a place where your thoughts are, *I have the power to change my life.*

Clear your mind from all the worries, concerns, and fears. Claim the Alpha status in your life. The Alpha status can only be reached when you are in a state of meditation. Determine your own way of relaxing your mind. You might try toning down the constant thinking and focus on your own breathing.

Get in touch with your true being. You are not a body with a soul. You are a soul with a body. However, the Ego dominates your body, emotions, and conscious thoughts. Reverse the roles and let your soul take control. Let the Ego serve you, not control you.

Look for ways to relax your mind, body, and soul. Take time to meditate or to take short walks to enjoy nature. You can take warm baths to just clear your mind of all stress. People visit wellness centers or get massages to de-stress themselves physically, mentally, and emotionally.

Once you are able to do this, you can empower your soul. When your mind is clear, you will be able to command the Ego to surrender its post. Once you have overpowered the Ego—the gatekeeper—you will have direct access to the blueprint.

Your subconscious mind is like a sponge, absorbing every emotion and thought you feed it. The blueprint will be moldable and the subconscious mind will be compliant. It will be prepared to take you to your journey towards accomplishing the master plan.

DISCOVERING YOUR BLUEPRINT — Preparation

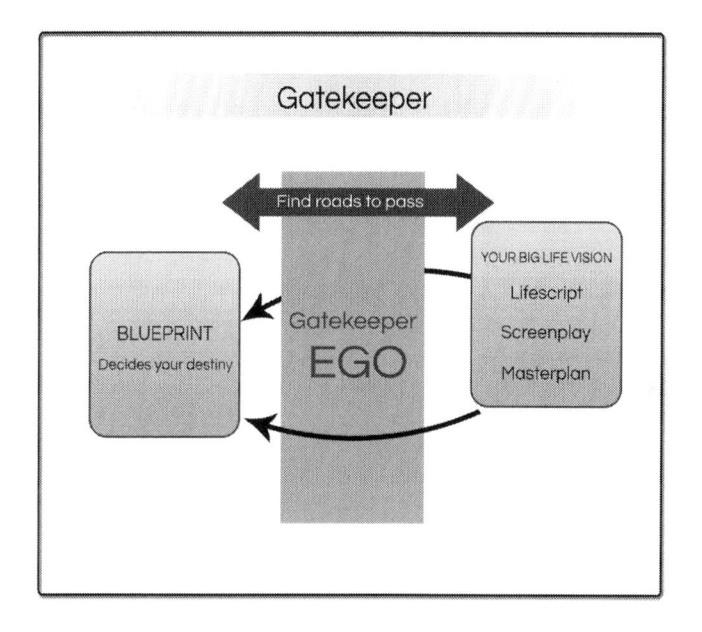

Figure 2: Gatekeeper

When you try to create your life vision and overwrite your blueprint, the Ego will act out to prevent you from doing so. The Ego serves as the gatekeeper to your blueprint. The Ego makes it difficult for you to overwrite your blueprint so that it can sync with your life vision and what you want to experience and manifest in your life. Nevertheless, despite the showdowns, you need to find the paths to overcome it. The intellectual mind is not the creator. The creator of your life vision is the blueprint, and the creator of the blueprint is you.

Poor Blueprint vs. Wealthy Blueprint

If you fail to access and transform your blueprint, it will remain the same in every circumstance. Think about how many lottery winners have lost their money in a short span of time. When people with a faulty blueprint win the lottery, their blueprint will take over; they will soon find that, as quickly as the money became theirs, it is gone. Their behavior toward the money ensures that they constantly fall back to their pre-lottery state of being. Remember Donald Trump? He had a blueprint of abundance. Despite losing billions of dollars due to faulty business deals, he was able to regain his money. People live according to the blueprint they allow regardless of how much money they have in the bank.

I personally experienced this truth after gaining a couple of million dollars by trading in the stock market. I had been operating in the fear of losing my prewritten blueprint. I was always anxious about the money, putting on a mask of success that was fixed in anxiety and paranoia. True to form, my blueprint caused all my money to be lost in a single day. It aligned my circumstances and conditions with what I felt and thought about. Accordingly, your subconscious state will work it out so that your internal and external conditions align.

You have the power and tools to change your blueprint. When you overwrite your negative blueprint, you can address whatever condition you're facing, whether relational, health, finance, emotions, or career. Everything is rooted in your blueprint.

Setting Your Emotional Mindset

To face your Ego in a showdown, your mind must be adequately prepared by setting it to an emotional level for success. Positive thinking is not enough; you cannot just think, "I can do it" without understanding why or how you have the power to do it. You can believe that you will be able to do it once you successfully change your blueprint and master plan. Changing these things empowers you to change the way you think, speak, and behave.

Give Your Emotions a Concrete Name

Emotions are so powerful that they dictate your behaviors. In a relationship, there will be times when you are angry with your spouse, and at such times, you will tend to give full vent to anger by saying hurtful things to your spouse. Likewise, when you're scared of something, you will probably avoid it like the plague.

If you feel fear or anger, you need to bring these emotions to the forefront and name them. When you bring something to light, you will be able to distinguish then extinguish it. You cannot master something that you can't name. When you name something, you can picture the emotion with a form. When something takes form, you can change it.

Your emotional mindset is the belief that you hold regardless of any evidence that may try to tear it down. What is something you believe about yourself? What has been dictating your blueprint? Once you establish an emotional mindset for empowerment, you will be able to use this to live a powerful life of fulfilling your purpose.

Do you believe you're not good enough? What emotions do these evoke? This belief likely creates feelings of inadequacy, frustration, and humiliation. These are powerful emotions. These emotions can prevent you from doing a lot of things in your life. Feeling inadequate will cause you to run away from opportunities. Feeling frustrated may cause you to stick with mediocre goals so that you won't be disappointed. Feeling despondent in your belief of not being good enough will cause you to isolate yourself. These feelings create a strong pull downward, and are highly detrimental to your well-being.

What if you reverse these feelings? What if you were to let go of the belief that you're not good enough and replace it with the belief that "I am willing to learn."? With this mindset, you will be willing to learn anything and everything. There's possibility and growth. We've all heard these concepts before, but there's a need to emphasize them so that our innermost beings can absorb the new beliefs.

Emotional Upgrade

Once you see progress, you can upgrade your expectations for your blueprint. You can set the emotional mindset to the belief that, "I am successful. Favor follows me wherever I go." What feelings will this claim evoke? If you believe you are successful and that favor follows you wherever you go, then you will feel excited, confident, and powerful—like you can do anything. You will feel that you can go out and fulfill your purpose. These emotions will then infuse you with purpose and drive to fulfill your soul's divine purpose.

Building and attaining your new blueprint is like a staircase. You take one step at a time, and when you find you accomplished that, you can build upon it knowing that you have succeeded in the past and will succeed as you take the next step. Don't let your emotional mindset cause you to stay downstairs, safe and small.

If a person doesn't grow, he is actually dying. People need to grow in order for everything else in their lives to grow. *We* need to grow so that we can grow our relationships, careers, businesses, and finances. In order to go to the next level, we need to get to a level of emotional maturity in which we can master our feelings. Only then, when we start to feel scared, doubtful or uncertain, can we turn these emotions around into feelings that will serve us rather than work against us.

EMOTIONAL BONDAGE THOUGHT PROCESS

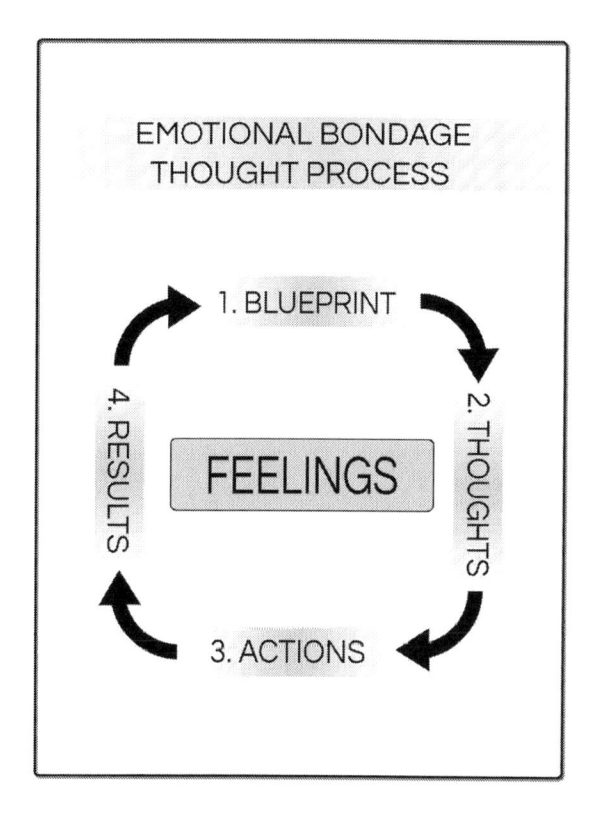

1. BLUEPRINT
2. THOUGHTS
3. ACTIONS
4. RESULTS

FEELINGS

Figure 3: Emotional Bondage Thought Process

When a person is stuck in emotional bondage, he will allow his feelings to lead his thoughts. If a person constantly has negative emotions, his blueprint can become destructive. Similarly, a person who has positive emotions creates a positive blueprint. In both situations, the person lets his emotions be the master of his thoughts and actions, which will, in turn, affect the outcome of his life. In the negative thought process, feelings guide life. That person is in emotional bondage, unable to control his thoughts, actions, and outcomes because of the lack of awareness of his blueprint and the Law of Attraction.

When you are aware of your blueprint as it is, you can dictate your thoughts and feelings in order to affect it and change it to how and what you want it to be. A lack of awareness of

Preparation | DISCOVERING YOUR BLUEPRINT

your blueprint causes it and your mindset to dictate wrong thoughts and feelings to you. Thus far, you have allowed your blueprint to be in control of you. Once you realize this, you must shift roles. *You* need to control your *blueprint*. *You* need to use it so that you can fulfill the master plan for your life. You are the only one who can take the control back.

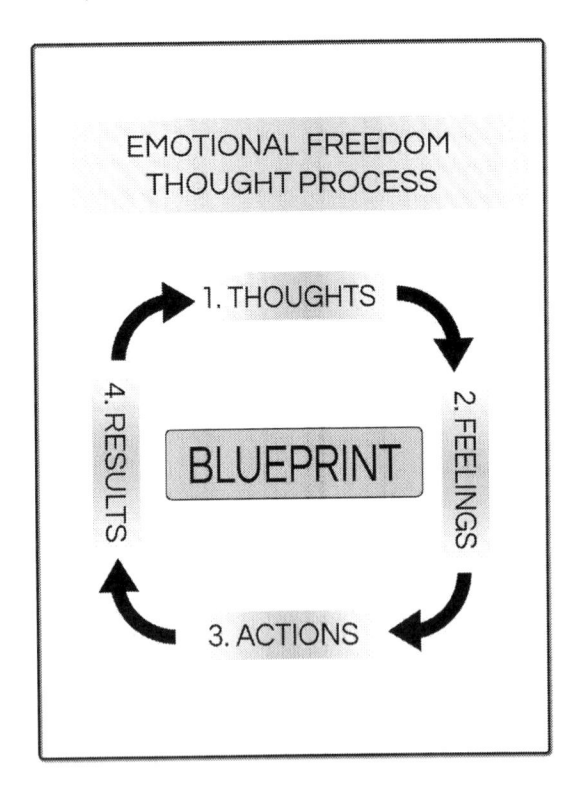

Figure 4: Emotional Freedom Thought Process

T. Harv Eker says that thoughts form feelings, feelings form actions, actions generate results, and results lead to new thoughts. In the center of the emotional freedom thought process, the blueprint, also known as the subconscious mind, powerfully affects the thought process. Through mastering your thoughts, you can guide your feelings to guide your actions to then create the outcomes you want in your life.

Preparing for Showdowns

When I left Zurich to go to Canada, my mind was consumed with the thought that when I returned I would know my true purpose in life. This was a decision I made as my mind transformed through reading and my eyes were opened to a whole new way of thinking. I thought to myself, *from now on my life is like a big experiment*. This statement released a lot of pressure that was an important part of opening myself to new experiences. Operating like a scientist, I proceeded with the experiment objectively. I opened myself up to all kinds of possibilities. I was about to either prove or disprove the Law of Attraction. I tried it out, and to my great surprise, it began to work for me.

I intended to move forward with a clean slate. I closed all the doors behind me and left Zurich with no idea of how I would fund my trip or if I would have a job to return to. On this journey, I committed to taking responsibility for all aspects of my life and to trust the Law of Attraction completely.

Taking Control of the Moment

When you decide to take control of your life and accept the challenge to take on the role as the master of your circumstances, you will certainly experience trials. But the difficult moments are merely physical manifestations of your Ego's resistance. Even if you're rationally making a move towards being in control, your Ego will resist and your subconscious mind will pick up on this as it manifests in your life.

I want to encourage you to press on in this new journey. These showdowns are an inevitable part of this journey, which proves that you're on the right path. They will reveal to you, and encourage you, that you have what it takes to operate as a master.

Generally, showdowns are tests; they are preparation for allowing you to receive what you want by testing your resolve to attain your vision. If you're not ready, you'll end up losing what you thought you wanted; along with the desire, there must be a commitment to receive what you want when it arrives. A lot of people pray for a lottery win without realizing that they're not ready to handle the responsibility that comes with wealth. This is why many of those who have won the lottery end up losing their millions within a few months or years.

People often have the notion that if they want something badly enough, they will receive it in the exact way they pictured it would happen, and *when* they want it to happen. Your role is only to declare what you want and then to trust that in the right time it will come; at the end of the day, despite appearances, it will manifest.

Don't Worry, Be Happy

Why does it matter how you will get it? Why worry how it's delivered to you if ultimately you will receive what you want? Imagine this scenario: you need money to pay rent. You declare what you need, believing that the rent will be covered. However, the showdown really begins when you're nearing the due date and the rent money has not appeared.

The nervousness you feel means that you doubt the Law of Attraction. Worry is a powerful emotion that overrides feelings of hope and trust. The key is to stay calm in these showdown situations. Staying calm shows that you have faith that the rent money will come at the right time. During these times of testing, you can focus your emotions on what it would feel like when you finally receive what you want.

Will you feel relieved and secure? Operate from this emotional mindset, and you will be closer to attaining your desires. Imagine with gratitude, as if what you're imagining has already been granted. Operate from a mindset of the future rather than the present. In doing so, you will summon the desired future into your present.

Have you ever experienced how things work out exactly when they need to? Money comes when you need it. Healing comes when you least expect it. Relationships are restored even before you've exerted effort to reconcile with your loved ones. These are breakthrough moments. In retrospect, they aren't that dramatic. The moments leading up to those points will likely be nerve-wracking, but this is the perfect time to practice mastering your emotions.

How I Received Confidence to Depart for Canada

When I left for Canada, I was under a contract to represent a financial service firm in Switzerland and Europe. Business dictated that it would be best to stay in Switzerland, but with the inception of the Internet, I was excited to test the communication possibilities by maintaining my professional services from a distance. No one knew I was going away because I did not want to thwart my personal development because of a job or money.

So I left without notice, without knowing how much time I would need to find my life's purpose. I started to embrace uncertainty. One morning I received a phone call from the owner of the group I represented. He was a very wise man and great mentor. When he called me I was already settling into my new home. I had to be upfront and let him know that I was no longer in Zurich.

Was I fearful that I was going to lose my job? Yes, this thought crossed my mind on several occasions, but I did not allow it to linger. I approached my next words from a peaceful place of thinking; it's all right if I lose my job. If this happened,

I was certain I would somehow be given a different source of income to fund the journey. I made the conscious decision that I would accept the consequences of my actions, and would be okay no matter what happened.

This job was my only source of income. I had no plan in place in case he would fire me. I just determined to trust. When I told him I was in Canada he was surprised, but responded with, "It's a beautiful place." He kept me on his payroll even though I was not in Zurich, giving me a life-changing opportunity for which I am ever grateful.

Rather than allowing my decisions to be based on somebody else's approval, I took control of how I was going to live my life. Without having a preordained outcome, I just made a decision for myself, knowing that it was what I needed to do. Somehow, I knew that this was the path I needed to take and listened to my intuition and my soul. Going to Canada was one of the most honest and groundbreaking decisions I have ever made. The decision gave me great emotional freedom and power to be able to follow through with the journey on which I'd set out.

We need to trust divine timing. We must be willing to go through the eye of a needle to get what we want; if we expect everything to be smooth sailing, we will back out at the first sign of conflict. Remember, showdowns are there to shake us up just enough so that we know that this is what we really want, and to show us that this is a path worth pursuing.

How I Received a Rent-Free Home

When I returned to Switzerland, I had no idea where I'd live. I had lost my condo unit. Here was another chance for me to test the Law of Attraction. Taking the opportunity offered and creating a picture in my mind of where I wanted to live, I determined that it would be a place that felt like perpetual vacation. Yes, I had to force myself to think and feel this. The LOA always delivers, but often sends trials your way to see if you are really trusting.

While trying to figure out my next course of action, I bumped into a friend. He asked me where I was staying during my house search, and then offered me his home while he went abroad to Thailand for a month. In exchange for looking after his home, I was able to live rent-free. I have come to believe that there are no coincidences in life. Your blueprint will manifest what you desire. It wasn't the vacation place I had dreamed about, but I took the opportunity in the way it was provided. Your desires will always be delivered to you somehow, even if they come in unexpected forms.

When he returned from his trip, we began discussing my journey to Canada. He had wanted to make some big changes in his own life. I arranged to stay awhile longer in his home in exchange for guiding him toward discovering his own purpose. If he were unsatisfied with the results, we would work out a different form of rent. My coaching career began quietly and unassumingly. If I couldn't help him, I would pay him.

For the next year and a half my inspiration and guidance led him to believe in himself. I had no formal coaching background at the time, but it worked. He had been employed as a social worker, but soon realized that he had a different master plan of becoming a teacher. In the same way, he helped me realize my true calling. He validated that part of my master plan was to coach people; guiding them toward pursuing and living the lives they've only ever dreamt of.

Don't Let Uncertainty Hold You Back

Discovering your master plan requires that you step out of your comfort zone. When you're acting like a slave of circumstance, you are still comfortable to some degree. You receive just enough of what you need while obeying the metaphorical masters in your life. You have structure and boundaries. But this is all you have. Your life is merely dictated to you.

When you decide to move forward, you will have to let go of your materialistic desires and worn-out relationships. The popular worldview suggests that in order to be happy, you must hold status and material possessions close to you.

However, the truth is that in order to be truly happy and emotionally free, you must overcome roadblocks of fear and uncertainty. Don't get me wrong—I like the capital markets and believe that markets serve us to live life in materialistic abundance, but the world places capitalism as the real purpose. It no longer serves you, but it places you in a submissive role of bowing before it. How can you change that? The secret lies within your value system. You don't need to follow every trend; instead, follow your inner voice. If you are no longer living by a materialistic worldview, you have no choice but to follow an inner path and accept uncertainty. Yes, you must learn to embrace it.

Embracing Uncertainty

The major thing that you must face is the concern that this endeavor might not work for you. It's understandable because you've been letting your Ego take control for the longest time and have never been in the driver's seat. You *can* make decisions; some of these decisions may not be 100-percent correct, but that's okay. At least, they are *your* decisions. You can modify them along the way.

You must first make the decision in your mind. You must approach it with the knowledge that this is good for you and that you have the power to see this through. You need to believe that your courage to step out of the rat race will be honored, and your sense of accountability will manifest in abundant ways.

People often have great ideas and visions, but they never start because the negative emotions get the best of them. Perfection is not the goal; action without fear is all that is asked of you. You don't need to flawlessly make your ideas into reality. You just need to move towards the reality you want one step at a time. It starts with the first step of acquiring your Ticket to Life. It's the first step in your journey toward experiencing the best quality life.

Letting Go of Past Limitations

If I had allowed the traumatic experience of losing my millions keep me from moving forward, then I would have gotten nowhere in life. I would have been paralyzed had I thought, *I lost all my money; what if it happens again?*

When domesticated elephants are young, their trainers tie down one of their feet with a peg. Try as they might, they cannot escape, so they stop trying. Elephants are said to have impeccable memories.

As these magnificent animals grow and mature, their trainers don't have to replace the peg that anchors their rope. Although the adult elephants now have the power to free themselves from the tiny peg holding them down, they recall that they had been unable to escape before, and so they never try again. Just like that, they give up; resigning themselves to the fate that this is life. The memory of failure in the past prevents them from striving toward freedom in the future.

Elephants and Us

This is how most adult humans operate. People who have spent their young lives being rejected, put down, and limited lose hope that they can ever amount to what they've always dreamed they could be. When we were young, life was full of possibility and hope. The blueprint of children is pure potential.

As these same little people grow up, their Egos take control. They experience life's realities that transform them into the conforming individuals that society desires. They may have tried a few times to escape, but after being unsuccessful, they stop trying and resign themselves to their fates. Our past experiences often put us on autopilot mode, thereby preventing us from operating outside of what has become the norm. Just like the elephants, adults avoid trying anything new because they believe nothing will come of it.

I'd Rather Be Rich Than Right

Years ago, I would rather have had a wonderful life than to be right about my beliefs being limiting to myself. What was I protecting? Most people protect *being* right. The Ego wants to be right all the time. It tells you, "You're no good," "You won't amount to anything," "You won't be rich", "You will have no real relationships," "You will fail". Because you've experienced this in the past, it doesn't mean that you will meet the same fate today. But, the Ego wants to be right.

> **TRANSFORMATION PRINCIPLE 4:**
>
> *In order to overwrite your blueprint, you need to be okay with being wrong.*

In order to overwrite your blueprint, you need to be okay with being wrong. You need to come to an honest place of admitting that you've been doing everything wrong all along. In order to free yourself from this cycle, you *must* try again. If, like the grown elephant, you refuse to try because of memories of past failures and the fear of history repeating itself, then now's the time to release those memories and start fresh. Try again. Shake yourself free. You can do it *this time*.

MENTOR'S SECTION: T. HARV EKER

Author of *Secrets of the Millionaire Mind* and *Speedwealth*, T. Harv Eker, is known as an expert in the field of financial success. He started out barely surviving as a businessman, but in two and a half years, Eker was able to turn his life around and became a successful millionaire, using the principles he teaches through his book and his seminars.

Eker experienced a tough childhood in Toronto, Canada. His parents struggled to make both ends meet. He needed to work at a young age of 13. He went through several odd jobs such as a newspaper delivery boy and an ice-cream scooper. He also worked at local fairs just to make money. When he studied at York University, his master plan to be a millionaire began to unfold.

When he had moved to the U.S., he worked on overriding his blueprint and he built it toward financial success. He started out a few business ventures, which did not work out, but he never wavered. He went to open one of the first retail fitness stores in the U.S., which grew from one to 10 branches in just two and a half years. He sold part of his company to a Fortune 500 company for $1.5 million. Eker eventually became successful in overriding the poor blueprint he had. In addition, he was able to turn his financial status around.

Eker uncovered that it was also a part of his master plan to help people see a different perspective about money and wealth. He helped people see how using a series of principles and techniques can change their blueprints.

One of his greatest influences in my life is the discovery that each person can change his or her blueprint to create wealth, becoming a multi-millionaire in the process. He was able to achieve these, so I was encouraged to go on my own path to discover and author my own blueprint and life script that brings about not only financial freedom but also emotional freedom that a lot of people take for granted.

> **Rich people believe "I create my life." Poor people believe "Life happens to me."**
>
> **– T. Harv Eker**

Chapter 4
The Universal Laws of Success

The Law of Attraction states that the universe responds to whatever you are offering—by giving you more of whatever you are vibrating. It doesn't care whether it is good for you or not; it simply responds to your vibration.

– Jack Canfield

The Power of the Media

When you hear horrible things happening through the news, you might feel nervous, anxious, fearful, or wonder what the world is coming to. There are far too many negative pictures and ideas in the news, which, when dwelt upon, seem to increase the frequency of similar events in your daily life.

News affects our day-to-day living in a variety of ways. At minimum, news drains our lives of any cheer or enthusiasm. Just watching already makes us increasingly disturbed.

In March 2014, a Malaysian Airline flight lost contact with its base and disappeared. The story gained worldwide attention because it was so bizarre to have a whole plane vanish. Authorities tried to explain the disappearance but have since failed to come up with leads. People everywhere felt distressed over the situation. The whole world was troubled about the lack of answers. The crash was reported in the news daily, flowing freely through the subconscious minds of many people across the world.

In July 2014, the world was to hear about another airplane crash, also a Malaysian Air flight. This happened at a time when the world's energy was focused on several news stories about airplane crashes. There had been too much negative energy surrounding the airlines, and particularly Malaysian Air. Was it coincidental that a plane from the same airline company was shot down over Ukrainian Sky? Could it have been that all the negative subconscious emotions from people all over the world came together and manifested in that crash? That is for you to determine.

Water is Water

A perspective shift is always needed to be able to supersede the natural tendency to continue in the rat race. No doubt that at some point disillusionment has led you to enter the seemingly inescapable maze that you've spent most of your life running in.

When you shift your perspective, you can begin to see these systems differently. What is a bottle of water worth to you? A dollar? That may be true in the city. But what does a bottle of water cost to a group of millionaires in the desert who have been walking for days and run out of water?

Thirsty and drowning in sweat, they would pay anything for some relief and hope for life. They would pay anything for that chance at life. Back in the city, no one would dream of paying more than $5 for a bottle of water, especially if they were near a convenience store. Water is water. Why is there such a difference between being in the desert and being in the city? It all boils down to the economic law of supply and demand: the greater the supply, the lesser the demand, the lesser the supply, the greater the demand.

Demand creates the value of any object. Whatever is in the market—water, gold, oil, or food—it is always priced according to the market's demand. It will be priced according to how scarce or abundant that particular object is in the area.

Most of the time, we view money as a limited supply. We operate from a place of lack or scarcity. We operate like the wealthy men in the desert, who are desperate for water. Anxiety takes over, and we become emotionally consumed by the need to acquire more money.

Coming from a Place of Abundance

At the end of the day, water is water, and money is money. You can come from a place of abundance. You can come from a place where you view that there is more than enough money to go around for everyone, just like there's more than enough water to go around for the people in the city. When you operate from this perspective and position, you will overwrite your blueprint. You will create a blueprint of abundance in which it doesn't matter what circumstance you find yourself in; you'll always *be* rich and so you'll eventually *have* riches.

Think about your emotional state when you buy bottled water from the store. You don't really think about it. You don't really feel threatened or worried that you won't be able to get any water. Somehow, you're assured that there will always be a supply of bottled water at the nearest grocery store.

How are your emotions different when you imagine yourself in the desert with no water supply? You would feel anxious and worried that you would die if you would not find water soon. When you're in the desert, you're emotionally unstable because you're already desperate for water. On the other hand, when you're in a convenience store buying water, you have the sense of stability.

The LOA and Your Blueprint

The LOA senses your emotional state. Your constant emotions shape your blueprint. When you're able to create emotional freedom, you will be able to come from a place of contentment. You know you've reached emotional freedom when you are capable of being happy for no reason. There's nothing in your circumstance that can change your state of happiness.

When you're emotionally free, you can come from a place of knowing that you will be abundantly provided for. You won't have a need to worry or be anxious. When you are emotionally free, you can create the blueprint of abundance and welcome a spectrum of good things into your life such as financial, relational, and spiritual abundance.

> **TRANSFORMATION PRINCIPLE 5:**
>
> **Reach emotional freedom before you can be financially wealthy.**

Getting Out of the Rat Race

When you are able to change your perspective of the monetary system, you can change how you feel about money. Instead of being in a rat race to acquire wealth, you can get and simply pursue your purpose in life; you can discover your own master plan. In the rat race, there will always be anxiety, discontentment, and frustration, and the LOA will work against you.

When you come from a place of inner abundance, you will have freedom in life. In this place, there will be no need to wear masks when your circumstances have no power over your emotions and you can simply become who you truly are.

When I attained the sense of constant inner peace, my life began to unfold in ways that I could never have imagined.

During that time, I felt that more and more of my life was coming into harmony and balance. I also felt happiness without any external reasons. Happiness is not like euphoria. It's just a constant feeling of calmness. This is not easy to describe but once you experience real happiness, you'll just know it. When I discovered these laws and surrendered myself completely to accomplishing my master plan, I sort of felt a new energy. For the first time in my life, I felt that I had constant connection to a power higher than myself.

Somehow you know that everything *will* be taken care of, even when you can't imagine how. For example, when I surrendered myself to this notion—that anything was possible and that I was safe—I discovered a new power and emotional strength that I couldn't have developed through my own intellect.

The Product of Worry and Fear

Before I started on this wonderful journey toward discovering myself, I was more fearful than happy. I operated in subconscious fear and worry, and allowed my Ego full control of my thoughts and emotions, rather than listening to my heart. At that time, I was unaware of the connection among heart, mind, and reality. I was controlled by intellectual thoughts because I didn't know any better. This journey taught me to master my thoughts and emotions, wherein I was able to operate in gratitude and hope. Coming from a place of joy, I experienced my emotions *and* circumstances transform in a noticeable way.

When the Ego is in control, fear and worry will be constantly present. The Ego wants you to fill the emptiness with temporary happiness, because not getting what it wants causes emotional pain. Fear is usually just a mere illusion.

We usually dwell on all the things that can go wrong, even when they do not yet exist. The more we think about those things, the more fearful we become of them actualizing, and the more they become our reality. When we operate in fear, we unknowingly invite the things we fear into our lives.

If you're worried or fearful, the key is to face your fear and think, *what's the worst thing that can happen to me?* When you imagine the worst thing, release yourself of the fear. Welcome these thoughts.

Visualize them as clouds that will come, but will soon pass. When you face your fears, they won't be as powerful a force as they once were in your life. Eventually, these fears can be replaced by feelings of excitement and joy.

The Value of a Master Plan and Life Script

Preparing your life script is important. It's more than just an activity for you to do on a rainy day—your life script will protect you through fear and anxiety. You can replace your thoughts of fear with prayers. You can replace them with a picture of what it's like to live out your master plan. With practice and commitment, you will find that when anxiety attacks, you can change your emotional state by focusing instead on the life script you have created.

The more you focus on your life script, the more it becomes real to you on an emotional and intellectual level. When this happens, you will see the LOA at work for you. You will see how little by little your reality will become a manifestation of your blueprint, and you'll be steps closer towards accomplishing your master plan.

THE ROUTER OF CONFIDENCE

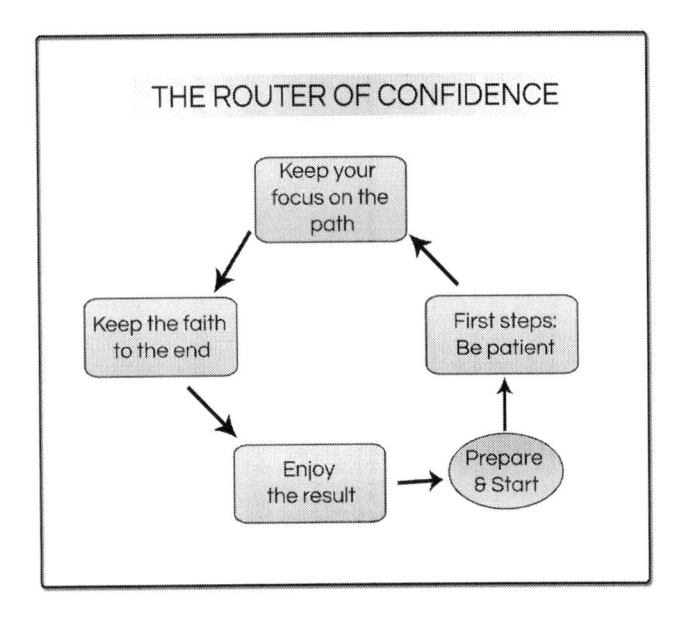

Figure 5: The Router of Confidence

The first steps toward doing anything is to prepare then take a step of faith and start it. You cannot get anywhere without preparation and starting. The first steps are often difficult and will require you to be patient. But even so, it's easy to become distracted. You will need to keep your faith until the life you designed manifests. As you enjoy the fruits of your faith, you can begin again with a new vision for your life.

Making the Shift

Before shifting your way of thinking from negative to positive, accept that your way of thinking has been hurting you. The LOA does not ask you if positive or negative thoughts cloud your mind; LOA doesn't filter them. You need to be careful about how you speak and how you think, even in playful banter.

For example, thinking, *Oh this will end up in disaster*, can be taken lightly, but this is taken as a command by the subconscious mind. You must allow yourself to feel guilty of acting inappropriately in the past when you did not know any better. Apologize and move forward.

From this point on, be intentional about speaking affirmations and positive things into your life. If you do so constantly, you'll experience a shift in the way you live your life. Being positive enables you to see the beauty in your life better.

The Emotional Feelings Barometer Chart below suggests that elevating your feelings by a point or so is already a huge improvement. However, you shouldn't force yourself when you are not able to reach completely good feelings about yourself. If you feel just a little bit better, this can make a huge difference. There's no rushing. One good thought at a time is progress.

Another advice I can give you is to get relaxed. Do something you enjoy like going to a wellness center, eating a good meal, playing sports, watching a movie, or meeting with good friends who can provide positive energy. You need to perform these activities since your goal does seem far-fetched. The experiment is not immediate; in addition, it will take practice to achieve.

Emotional Condition Barometer

High Frequency
You manifest unconscious abundance and wealth

OPTIMUM LEVELS — **10** — Performance, Love

7 — Faithful

5 — Inspirational, Confident

2 — Experimental, Motivated, Thankful

NEUTRAL — **0** — Constant calmness, Neutral

-2 — Frustration, Anger

-5 — Sorrow, Pessimism

-7 — Fear, Guilt

RESTRICTED LEVELS — **-10** — Depression

Low Frequency
You manifest unconscious emptiness and losses

Awareness of the Law of Attraction / *Emotional Condition*

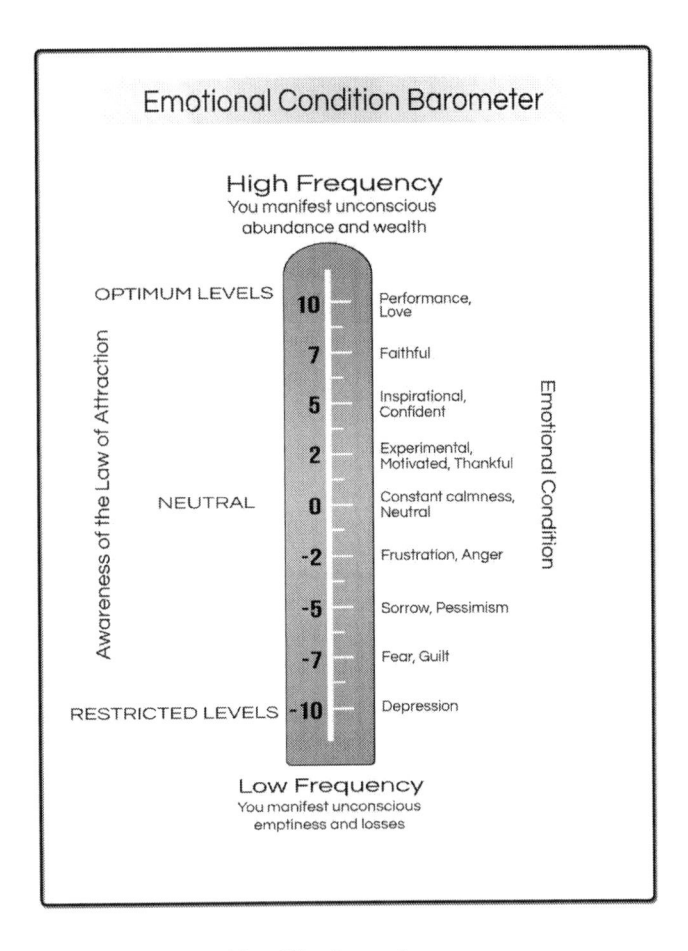

Figure 6: Emotional Condition Barometer

Inspired by Roy Martina's *The Missing Link* book, this figure depicts the different outcome when you have emotional freedom versus emotional bondage. When you have emotional freedom, you will manifest abundance and wealth. But emotional bondage will push you to manifest emptiness and loss in your life. When you are aware of the Law of Attraction, you'll realize the importance of your emotional state. Most people start out depressed and fearful with intense feelings of guilt. Your emotions will go up the emotional barometer from low-frequency emotions to high-frequency. The more you know about the LOA, the more your emotional condition will improve until you reach the emotions that are best suited for performance and love. These are optimum levels for manifesting abundance and wealth. Emotional freedom leads to financial success.

Waiting Game

The thing about the LOA is that results never happen overnight. Our current situations are products of our constant thoughts. Most people try to operate by the LOA but they lose faith when they don't receive immediate results. They have the tendency to think, *this isn't true because it doesn't work for me*. To be empowered by the LOA, you need to be constantly aware of your thoughts and words; you also need to be patient. The LOA is a waiting game, and in this game, the one who patiently waits wins.

> ***TRANSFORMATION PRINCIPLE 6:***
>
> ***The LOA is a waiting game, and in this game, the one who patiently waits wins.***

Be Able to Delay Gratification

People could get impatient to wait for what's best. Being so, they settle for immediate gratification that brings about temporary satisfaction. However, they could end up feeling empty and unsatisfied. In contrast, patiently waiting for good to come is likely to yield best outcomes.

Shifting from Victim to Master

Can we humans truly control our lives? Or are we all just a drop in the great ocean of life? Looking at the world, it's easy to think that we are victims of circumstance. Unemployment, poverty, sickness, depression, and dissatisfaction are all around the world. All these woes strengthen the idea that we are victims of circumstance in a constantly spiraling world.

All your life, you might have been focusing on the wrong things. You might have been stuck living your life as a slave instead of mastering and authoring your destiny. In the history of humanity, people have faced nearly impossible situations, which they overcame. Accordingly, man is responsible for what he is, and being so, he has the power to control his circumstances and to create circumstances for his upward climb.

The slave is unsure of how to create circumstances that he desires. He often thinks that what happens to him is caused by everything else. Nothing seems to be created by his personal choices or decisions. And so, he blames heredity, the environment, and every other external thing as reasons for his failures. He views everything to come out from his natural limitations as a person.

The master, on the other hand, searches into the mysteries of human life. He discovers a wonderful world of power, possibility, and promise. He tells us that the mind is the creative cause of all things. He also recognizes that personal conditions result from his actions, which are direct outcomes of his own ideas and feelings manifested as reality.

Plans and ideas are so powerful that they cause the good, bad, or indifferent things in one's life. Thoughts and feelings are able to influence external conditions. Given that, the master understands that when he taps into the power of the mind, he creates a happy and satisfying experience that can last a lifetime.

As was pointed out, we are the designer and builder of our lives. We create something from within (an idea) before materializing it on the outside. The truth is that all fears of poverty, sickness, and loneliness start as impressions and mental pictures before they turn into painful realities. Whether the picture is good or bad, the Law of Attraction will bring it about since it does not question or challenge the kind of picture we provide; it simply proceeds to materialize the mental picture into a visible reality.

When Thoughts Become Reality

When you think of things according to your master plan and experience such thoughts emotionally, then you command these thoughts to become your reality.

Some of us think that it's impossible for us to actualize our thoughts about the things we want for our lives. But our blueprints can create anything, and by constantly meditating on our life script, we can shape our blueprint into commanding the situations we want it to create. In this way, our master plan becomes a reality.

When I left the corporate world to start my own business, I faced a lot of uncertainties. Starting my asset management company, I had to raise an initial two million dollars, which seemed impossible. I was worried about who would take interest to invest their money in my company because they didn't know my company or me. But while I thought of that, I also imagined what it would be like if investors came to me with this kind of money. I did cold calls. I went out to talk with people. I *believed* it would happen though I didn't know *how* it would happen. However, I operated under a mindset that made me believe my plan was a possibility. In a couple of months, I was able to raise the needed amount. Needless to say, I commanded the universe to deliver two million dollars for the asset management firm, and it did.

MENTOR'S SECTION: RHONDA BYRNE

Rhoda Byrne is an Australian television and film producer who became the mastermind of the self-help novel, *The Secret*. In 2004, Byrne experienced an emotional breakdown because of personal and professional problems. In the process of dealing with her woes, Byrne discovered the secret that has long been in existence since the beginning of humankind, but that it was not widely known nor practiced. That secret changed her life.

As she unearthed the power of the Law of Attraction, Byrne felt it was her duty to share this message with the world. Reading Byrne's book *The Secret* allows a person to come into terms with his potential and purpose in life. The book also helps readers to identify and grasp the power they have over their own lives.

Byrne's inspiration for writing the book was a research that she herself did. The research was on the most influential people and the highest achievers of all time such as scientists, artists, innovators, musicians, and pioneers. *The Secret* opened up my mind to the significance of pursuing purpose, rather than wealth. The secret also led me to build my life towards my master plan and life script.

> "Be grateful for what you have now. As you begin to think about all the things in your life you are grateful for, you will be amazed at the never-ending thoughts that come back to you of more things to be grateful for. You have to make a start, and then the Law of Attraction will receive those grateful thoughts and give you more just like them."
>
> — Rhonda Byrne

Part II
Stand Still, Endurance, & Healing

The best way to understand the foregoing chapters is to compare them to caterpillar's metamorphosis into a beautiful butterfly. Currently, you might be a caterpillar running around in relationships with other caterpillars, but remember that you yourself are a butterfly who can fly freely and enjoy a lifestyle different from that of a grounded caterpillar. In a bigger context, it's your decision in which worldview you like to live, but like what I did back then, you may decide to develop all essentials and enjoy the new feeling of a light and good prospect life.

To become the unique butterfly, which matches your inner self, you must go through a period which many people fear. But like the insect inside the cocoon, you must endure this "fearsome" period, during which you are defenseless and vulnerable. In this period, your old hurt feelings can be transformed if you will allow them to. In your imaginary cocoon, you will experience a spotlight on your hurt feelings, which may be put on a final hurting, and then healing begins.

The process of transformation is normal if you compare it to an operation. During the said period, all your hurting feelings brought by the past, and even those that have been wrongly guiding your life, need to be healed. So while you're still in the cocoon, you have to be patient and humble.

If at times you feel everybody even by God is leaving you out then it's time to consider that feeling untrue. In fact, you are protected as you begin to give up resistance. The same protection will also guide you in the process of metamorphosing yourself into a beautiful flying butterfly for the rest of your life.

The succeeding chapters will connect you to the aforesaid period. May I say, however, that this period may seem bleak or gloomy at certain points, but that cannot be avoided because I went through the same stage. While you're in your imaginary cocoon, you must be able to start healing and getting strong to unwrap yourself with no help from outside.

You need to develop inner strengths and have the confidence that you can take the process yourself. As the change happens, you must also keep guided by your life vision and master plan, especially when you start doubting yourself. In addition, you need to begin letting go of the wrong belief systems or misleading relationships that have since distracted you from the true way. The process is perilous, like being rocked around like a boat in a huge storm, but you will be assured you'll be able to weather the storm. This is your permit to captain your life

Chapter 5
Look in the Mirror

"What is a teacher? I'll tell you: it isn't someone who teaches something, but someone who inspires the student to give of her best in order to discover what she already knows."

— Paulo Coelho

The Man in the Mirror

My realization over the need to remove my masks and wrongly guided emotions led me to Canada. Deciding to leave for Canada, I knew that my life was about to change if only I would let of all the habits and mindsets that had been dictating over my entire life. During that time, I had to be completely honest with and face myself who I really was. I am sure you have experienced the same woes; I am sure, too, that you have wondered if you could be free one day.

Facing the Music

The most difficult part of the journey was my reservation to share what and how I felt and who I was behind the masks. In contrast, I can now look in the mirror and see myself staring back at me; it's no longer the stranger who used to appear in the mirror whenever I looked in it. Having gone through the process, I can completely understand why most people have difficulty of changing their habits and worldviews.

Often, people's loneliness and despondency keep them in the same status quo, which they consider as the totality of life. They are afraid to move into the unknown territory since they have lived their entire life in the shadow of a perceived safety. But what they obtain in "safety" they lose in bondage to emotions and fears.

Accordingly, I had difficulty in recognizing and accepting that I had been living my life behind a mask of fear. However, I now concur that that difficulty was completely necessary. Yes, the heartache was utterly real, but considering what I have become, it was only temporary.

The internal struggle, in the process, ceased when I realized that I had within me the key to the door where the power to enable me to overcome my greatest fears was waiting. Generally, each of us has this power as it is built into our blueprint. In my case, I used this power to overwrite my blueprint of fear with one of courage and self-acceptance. This goes to show that it is only when you take off your mask—not with positive thinking or outside activities—that real transformation can begin. It's an inner journey, which can be both frightening and healing, like cleaning old skeletons out of the closet.

The Cost of Living Life Unexamined

Another point I would like to make concerns self-awareness, which we often take for granted. It is not correct that we constantly ask why we have to know more about ourselves or what is there to know thinking that we have spent our lives being 'I'. Asking these questions does not enable us to go into the deepest corners of our being. When we do so, we miss out on the beauty and the freedom that self-awareness can bring.

The lack of self-awareness makes us worried on a daily basis. It also produces a failure to act, because instead of doing so, we just tend to react. This especially occurs when we are nervous and unfocused, when the state of mind gets stuck in a constant urgency. The resulting stress can be a killer.

When you operate in aforesaid manner, you will tend to experience burnout and depression. When you're unaware of your life, worry is sure to ensue. This is because we find ourselves with negative thoughts resulting in negative emotions, and ultimately, negative blueprints.

If we know ourselves, we will understand our very purpose. Otherwise, we will fail to believe in a higher power. We will feel the need to bear everything on our own shoulders.

Curing Burnouts

Imagine driving a car with the handbrake up. You may think you're getting somewhere, but little by little, your tires will wear out. It takes so much power and gas to drive this way, but you won't get very far. Soon enough, your car will break down. You may think, "Why in the world would I drive with my handbrake up?" Accordingly, a lot of people live their lives like this simply because they don't know their handbrakes are up.

Media and society have influenced us to think it's okay to pretend to be someone we're not in order to fit in. When you have masks, you will pursue things that aren't genuinely important to you. These masks make your blueprint operate in an inauthentic manner, resulting in burnouts in life. These burnouts can only be cured when you focus on the true path. Additionally, they can be cured when you realize that your handbrake is on, hence you can finally set yourself free to pursue a life you want.

More specifically, burnouts are produced by our wrong priorities, which are usually signs of your lack of self-awareness. Once you discover your blueprint and master plan, priorities will fall into place. Furthermore, when you discover more and more of your plan and purpose in life, your priorities become clearer. In contrast, hiding behind a socially accepted behavior results in the need to pursue things that aren't really important. You only get to do so to keep up with the act and to satisfy your Ego.

Getting off the Rollercoaster

Your life's purpose is to fulfill your own master plan. However, you also need to fulfill this plan with the help of a higher power. You cannot do it by yourself. While working as a banker, I allowed my feelings and behavior to be determined by external factors. When I didn't reach my financial goals, I became depressed. When I made a lot of money, I would enter a temporary state of euphoria, but it didn't last very long.

Most people can probably relate to this rollercoaster of emotions, which, come to think of it, is a detriment to their well-being. This rollercoaster crashes into what feels like a crumbling world leaving them powerless because every hope is placed on their circumstances. This, therefore, confirms that the lack of awareness can leave you feeling stuck and out of control every time. In as much as I have got to understand what a stable emotional life can look like, which I call 'inner peace', I believe you, too, can obtain the same understanding.

The Freedom of Self-Awareness

As has been said, living a life without self-awareness enslaves you to circumstance. The only weapon to address this issue is self-awareness, which is the key to freeing yourself.

Self-awareness will enable you to let go of emotional and materialistic products that have been dragging you down. It will also prove that material things and external factors cannot measure true happiness.

> **TRANSFORMATION PRINCIPLE 7:**
>
> **True self-awareness empowers you to detach yourself from everything that keeps you stuck and limits your movement.**

Detaching yourself from negative behaviors will help you become connected with everything in such a way that the entire universe will be your resource. Self-awareness is the experience of feeling synchronized with the power inherent in every living thing. It will allow you to move forward and create outcomes for yourself toward becoming a master of your life.

When you see yourself for whom you truly are, you also become aware of all your limitations and weaknesses. You will come to terms with your limitations and weaknesses and learn to accept them because life is not lived based on one's strength only—these negatives are part of the system.

Self-awareness results from the connection between yourself and your master plan. It sets in when you feel free and blessed, eventually leading to your understanding of your life's purpose. Your succeeding actions will be filled with new purpose. Consequently, you will start to live in the moment, for today.

Breaking Free

When you realize that you no longer want to be a slave to circumstance, you begin to look for something that will cause your life to transform radically. The more you go forward without fear, the more you discover whom you really are.

Through this discovery, you will find yourself changing some habits. For example, instead of waking up with a "Can I just stay in bed today" attitude, you will wake up with a feeling of excitement. You will look forward to the day and the experience it will bring. That and other beautiful things will make you feel that life is an exciting adventure. When you're able to feel this, the LOA reacts to your blueprint, hence making excitement and gratitude manifest themselves. When you live like this, you live in freedom. That was what I had been longing for my entire life.

The Universal Law of Identity

Living in self-awareness translates to living in accordance with the Universal Law of Identity. The Universal Law of Identity states that everything that exists has a specific nature. In the same way, self-awareness allows you to be true to who you are (your nature) and to your individual gifts. Judgment and comparisons are unnecessary because self-awareness enables you to know who you are. Who you are is a person of his or her blueprint and a script to influence his or her living.

Your life becomes more meaningful when you recognize its purpose. The more you understand who you are, the more you will become conscious of that purpose. Living purposefully will fill you with light and happiness that's free from external circumstances.

Part of my master plan is to be a life-transformation coach. By being so, I can serve my fellows who want to attain inner peace and emotional freedom. Whenever I reach out to people for said concern, I feel an extraordinary sense of fulfillment. In so doing, I enable myself to become who I was meant to be.

Following my example, you will lose the fear of consequences. People are unable to take off the masks because they're afraid of the uncertainty that this would create in life. Losing this fear allows you to express yourself authentically in your pursuits. The freedom that comes with authenticity is priceless. It is like deciding to remove the mask, and letting a huge weight lift off. You will have to do that so you will be able to live a life of integrity and honesty. Only then can you restore the workability in your life.

The Link between Integrity and Workability

Let me illustrate workability? When a table is missing one leg, it will trip. The table won't "work" the way it is supposed to work since it's incomplete. Integrity pertains to being complete or whole. When a table is missing one leg, it lacks integrity as a table; therefore, its purpose is defeated. Do you now see how a table that lacks integrity will also lack workability?

Similarly, when something about us is inauthentic, our life just won't "work". We lack integrity if we choose to live a life of incompleteness. All of us were born essentially complete, but render our lives incomplete by taking on behaviors that we may equate to money and status.

In addition, when our words and actions do not reflect our true beings authentically, then we also lack in integrity. Of course, when we have masks, we lack integrity, and therefore our lives lack workability.

Because you are only a beginner, people who have attained freedom and live as butterflies with integrity will immediately recognize who you are. You cannot play your game with them and wear your masks. They will see right through it all.

Embracing vulnerability

Discovery and adherence to the master plan will enable you to be the unique person you have always been within you. Apparently, you don't have to live in pretense, depending on who happens to be around you at any given moment, when you have discovered that unique person in you. In some sense, doing this may yield some fear, especially because you have been used to considering how people will react. But you must remember that putting off masks makes a person vulnerable; it exposes your true self. However, true strength comes from your ability to be vulnerable, and, to a certain degree, to be okay with that vulnerability.

In being vulnerable, you love yourself enough to let the whole world see you for who you are, without pretenses and facades. So when you put down the masks, you also decide to not get affected by the opinions and standards. Moreover, the judgment of the world, because it no longer matters to you, can no longer define you.

When you lay down your mask, you free yourself from the pressure of external factors. It signifies that you have found a new power in living your life for yourself. This is when you take on the responsibility for designing your own blueprint and discovering your own master plan. At the end of the day, this is what each one of us wants to experience, isn't it? We want to have the freedom to truly become ourselves.

The Illusion of the Mask

The masks we wear represent our comfort zones, but our masks offer only empty promises to keep us safe within the boundaries of a predefined status quo. The only thing it our comfort zones offer is a time-bred familiarity that allows us to live behind a false identity. Because of this familiarity, we have become oblivious to taking off our masks. But when we come face-to-face with the mirror and see the reflection looking back at us, we realize that all this time we have been inauthentic. This mirror represents our troubles, which we will only recognize when external factors come to shake us and take us back to the reality. We then realize that we have been wearing masks and merely playing roles. We have been pretending to be people we're not in order to fit in a system.

When trying times come, we realize that our masks are no longer enough. For some time, they've served their purpose, which is to hide our fears. But like any secret in this world, our mask will find a way to reveal itself. Well, nothing can ever be kept hidden. Therefore, you need to accept that your masks no longer serve their purpose. Take them off.

You shouldn't fear the results for putting down your masks. According to a previous statement, there's nothing to fear in vulnerability. That is, when you face your fears, you will no longer need these masks to keep you hidden.

Giving up the Reins

Some people have a hard time letting go of their reins when they're faced with uncertainties. They think that doing so will eventually render them helpless. But that misconception is just pointless. In fact, the secret to letting go of those reins is to trust some power beyond yourself. Therefore, giving up your masks means giving up the need to compensate for your weaknesses since after all that compensation is not the point. The missing link in your life that has rendered you unfulfilled is your relationship with a higher power. It is the same higher power that placed you where you are to be someone special.

I know a man who was imprisoned in Brazil. While he was in jail, he intently prayed for God to get him out of there. When he got out and returned to Switzerland, he came back to living the way he always had. He forgot about God.

Does this sound familiar to you? During difficult moments, do you call on a higher power for help? Truly, it is in dark moments when we can admit our own weakness and need, admitting that there is no other way but to seek someone's help. But when all our woes dissipate, we get back to being in control. We put our masks back and go on living as if we don't need anyone's help to survive.

Taking an Honest Look

A while back, I said that a mirror could represent the troubles that we encounter in our life. This time, I urge you to look in the mirror and take an honest inventory of whom we are. However, taking such self-inventory isn't possible without you being aided. The realization that you can't do it by yourself is both humbling and empowering. It is humbling because you realize that you've been trying to do it by yourself for the longest time. However, it's empowering because the burden to perform and to "have it all together" is removed given that all we need to do is to "order" and the universe will "deliver."

A Biblical verse says, "Therefore I tell you, whatever you ask in prayer, believe that you have received it, and it will be yours" (Mark 11:24, New International Version). During my stay in Canada, I read the Bible in the hope of looking for answers. In the verse, we see no pretensions, no desperation, and no competition. There's only the act of asking, of being in faith, and of receiving. This is what putting down your mask is all about.

Touched by an Angel

I came to a point in my life when I felt I was ready to surrender it all. I willingly prayed in desperation for help. I got an answer that I never expected at just the right time. I was in a wellness center one evening, enjoying some relaxation to clear my mind of everything. Suddenly, I felt something shifted in the atmosphere. I could almost *feel* someone in the room. My mouth went dry and I felt as if somebody's hands were on my shoulders.

In my spirit, I heard a loud and clear voice saying, "I am the archangel Michael, and I now take control of your life; let go and do what you're supposed to do. Don't worry any longer—just trust me." And then there was silence. But I felt he was still there. He spoke again, "Do you have any questions?"

I was caught completely off-guard. The experience was surreal, but I managed to say, "Yes, just one. Is there anything I need to do?" It was all I could think of to ask. Looking back to the experience, I can tell you that when you find yourself with a heavenly being, your posture and your heart's attitude shift in such a way that you're humbled. When you're humbled, all you want to do is serve and surrender yourself.

The archangel answered: "Tell others about this experience. Write a book about your life. Be honest, even if people laugh at you, avoid you, or call you insane. Trust me and I will protect you in every phase of your life." What came next was complete silence. I asked if he was still there, but there was no response. But I knew that it was a turning point in my life. After that night, I knew my prayers had been answered through an angel. I knew this angel was sent to give me security in the fact that I was indeed on the right path.

Archangel Michael

I'm not an expert on angels, or spirituality, by far. I just like to share my stories of transformational experiences. Now, I want to stay true to my word—that I would recount my angelic experience. That all-important experience revealed to me that some things in this world are beyond our understanding and power. To understand them, though, we just need to trust. We need to have faith to be able to experience a true sense of joy and peace transcending all understanding.

Michael the archangel guards the physical realm. He is stationed here to help humanity grow and to empower us to live our lives of abundance. He oversees the other guardian angels that collectively help us to release our fears and worries. They surround us in magical ways so we can open ourselves up to true experiences of love. They operate so we can discover our master plan.

Angels are all around us, ready to help. All we need to do is to invite them into our lives and they will connect with us. They're not limited by time and space. As we take off our masks and become vulnerable, we need not fear anything. Angels are there to protect us; hence, given that, we actually understand that we will not survive on our own.

The more you open yourself up to a higher power, the more you will feel connected to everything, and the closer you will come to being *you*. That is the point in which you will experience inexplicable peace and joy. By then, that same angel-hand that rested on my shoulder years back is also resting on your own shoulder. Yes, something like that could happen to you, too; all you have to do is to let go and have faith.

Only in our humility to accept our vulnerabilities and to acknowledge a higher power can we truly experience real results in our lives. The missing link in the journey of most people is not their *knowledge* of the LOA; it is the acknowledgment of a higher power empowering them, guiding them, and protecting them along the journey. But as you let go of the illusion and the mask, you will finally connect to the truth that there is more power in the world than meets the eye.

Fasten Your Seatbelt

The first thing you do when you enter your car is to fasten your seatbelt. That is because you want to be secure during the driving, but you're prepared for the worst. So, does fastening your seatbelt mean you fear crashing so you eventually decide to not drive your car anymore? No. You put on your seatbelt, aware of the risks and dangers in driving a car. But you still put that key into the ignition and you start the engine. You can't let fear keep you from driving your car.

In the same way, you can't allow fears to keep you from living your life well. You can't allow fear to win by keeping you from taking off your masks. The best you can do is to prepare for the worst. So put on your seatbelt and drive your car with wisdom.

When you put down your mask, things will change. That's the point, isn't it? You don't want more of the same. You want to break the status quo in your life - thus far, it has only kept you limited and powerless.

Instead of fearing the uncertain, you can actually live preparing for it. For example, you can prepare for changing relationships. Prepare to lose all the fake relationships, and alongside that, prepare to lose the things you don't need in your journey. Prepare to lose all the unimportant things because they tend to slow you down from actualizing your goals. So fasten your seatbelt, it will be an amazing ride.

MENTOR'S SECTION: PAOLO COELHO

Paolo Coelho is one of the most successful authors of our generation. In fact, he holds the Guinness World Record for the most translated book by a living author. What most of us don't know is that did not always look as if Coelho would become the celebrated author that he is today. Born in Brazil, Coelho always wanted to be a writer, but his mother did not want him to be a writer; she wanted him to be an engineer like his father. Coelho's determination to become a writer led his parents to enroll him in a mental institution. He escaped thrice, and was finally released when he was 20.

To please his parents, he enrolled in law school. But that was not the purpose of his life. Eventually, he left because the passion for writing never really left him. He left Brazil and traveled to South America, North Africa, Mexico, and Europe. In one of his trips, Coelho walked more than 500 miles the Road of Santiago de Compostela in Northwestern Spain, an event that changed his life and awakened his spirit. Admittedly, Coelho's life is a big influence to me. It resonated with me.

Sometimes, society and family have their own expectations for the person we'll become and the jobs we're supposed to have. However, it takes a leap of faith so that we can finally set out to be the person we've always desired and longed to be.

> **I learned long ago that in order to heal my wounds, I must have the courage to face up with them.**
>
> **- Paulo Coelho**

Chapter 6
Follow Your Joy

It is only with the heart that one can see rightly; what is essential is invisible to the eye.

Antoine de Saint-Exupery

What makes you happy?

I can still remember how strangely I felt when I looked in the mirror and saw a lost man staring back at me. I saw a man who had realized he could no longer live the way he had been living his life for the longest time. I saw a man who allowed his job, relationships, money, and status to define him. But at the time I was looking at him, I was sure that man had decided to strip himself of all that he held dearly. I saw a man who was at a standstill; he was uncertain if he should return to the corporate world or pick up the shreds of courage and move forward to follow his desires.

To be able to discover yourself and walk toward your joy in life, you must give up what gave you short-term benefits and made your life dull and miserable, in fact. In the process, you will see that the tiniest things are likely to cause unhappiness. A little rain, an argument, a bad day at the office, or poor health is enough to cause some depression. But you see your life will be incessantly unhappy if you continue to live the way you did in the past, causing you burdens due to the responsibility you placed on the external factors in search of true happiness.

In my experience, I discovered that in order to be truly happy, I needed to look within—it is where true happiness emanates. Looking within me, I had to cut cobwebs and skeleton-filled closets; it was fearful yet liberating. Through that unique journey, I learned that I am responsible for my own emotions and that my emotions do not depend on external circumstances or on other people. I also learned that living my life that way resulted in elation and deflation happening as a cruel, never-ending cycle. But when I decided to take off the masks, I began to distinguish between temporary and stable causes of happiness, illusionary versus real sources of joy. The moment I decided to that, I knew I was experiencing genuine transformation.

Emptying Yourself Out

Imagine a bowl full of water. Can you pour soup into that bowl with water? Of course not, the bowl will overflow. It won't be able to accommodate any new content since it's filled with something else.

Similarly, to receive pure joy in your heart is impossible when your heart itself is filled with negative emotions like worry, fear, anxiety, and resentment. In a bigger context, you cannot form empowering beliefs to override your blueprints when you're still holding on to limiting beliefs. The thing is that opposite beliefs are impossible to have simultaneously; therefore, you need to let go of one, so that you can welcome the other.

> **TRANSFORMATION PRINCIPLE 8:**
>
> *You need to let go of negative emotions and beliefs so that you can create an open space in your life for joy and boundless possibilities.*

You need to let go of negative emotions and beliefs so that you can create an open space in your life for joy and boundless possibilities. Not letting go of these negative emotions would mean that you'd continue living in deceit. You'll only by able to experience joy and peace deep within if you let go of your fears and the worries. You simply need to make room in your heart for the emotions that will work for you. Once you let go of limiting beliefs, you will realize that there's a whole world of possibilities out there just waiting to happen.

One of these limiting beliefs is that which enslaves you to circumstance. Remember that you are responsible for your emotional freedom, and being so, you are the only one who can generate joy into your life. You cannot continue depending on others for happiness; in that way, you also continue fooling yourself under the guise of undergoing transformation. Indeed, you need to give up all your past illusions of life and happiness for change to occur.

What Makes You Truly Happy?

What areas of your life give you illusory happiness? Is it by remaining in a dysfunctional relationship? Well, I've been there, and I can tell you it doesn't work that way. I can't force someone to love me. Although it was difficult, I had to empty myself of all expectations of loving and being loved by someone. I had to decide to have love within myself as the author of the emotions I wanted.

In addition, my attempts at seeking family approval for creating happiness were also futile. No doubt, if you are honest with yourself, you will discover that the kind of joy that you have considered real is actually completely inauthentic.

Looking back, I used to drive a nice car, live in a nice condo, and had a pretty penny tucked away in the bank. It looked like a pretty great and happy life. But over the years, I realized that the 'joy' was only a façade; it was a temporary respite from trying to please the people around me. Far too quickly, that "joy" brought me to the saddest and lowest point in my life. I realized that externally-based contentment will always be revealed for what it is—an impostor.

Detachment

Nothing can rule your life unless you give it the reins. That is what we generally do, though. In my experience, I realized that true happiness could only become real if I detached myself from external factors and feelings. In the process, I saw the lie I had been living. Seeing it meant I didn't need anything to be happy.

The Bible says, "Seek first his kingdom and his righteousness, and all these things will be given to you as well" (Matthew 6:33). This passage reveals the need to seek your master plan to understand your blueprint and how you operate. Eventually, when you find yourself running in emotional freedom, the good—such as financial freedom—will manifest.

> **TRANSFORMATION PRINCIPLE 9:**
>
> *Pursuit of a higher purpose will free you from attachment to the material world and wealth.*

To attain financial freedom, one generally tends to run in circles after material wealth and to operate out of desperation and materialism. Given that, it's important to remind yourself of the power and influence of your emotions on your circumstances and conditions. Instead of learning to control circumstances and driving yourself crazy, learn instead to control your thought life. Taking charge of thoughts and emotions will lead to you freedom.

ATTITUDE FOR WEALTH

	ATTACHMENT	DETACHMENT
ORGANIZATIONAL STRUCTURE	Employee/Plays security	Business Owner/Plays teamwork
INDEPENDENCE	Self-employed/Plays solo	Investor and Trader/ Plays emotional freedom

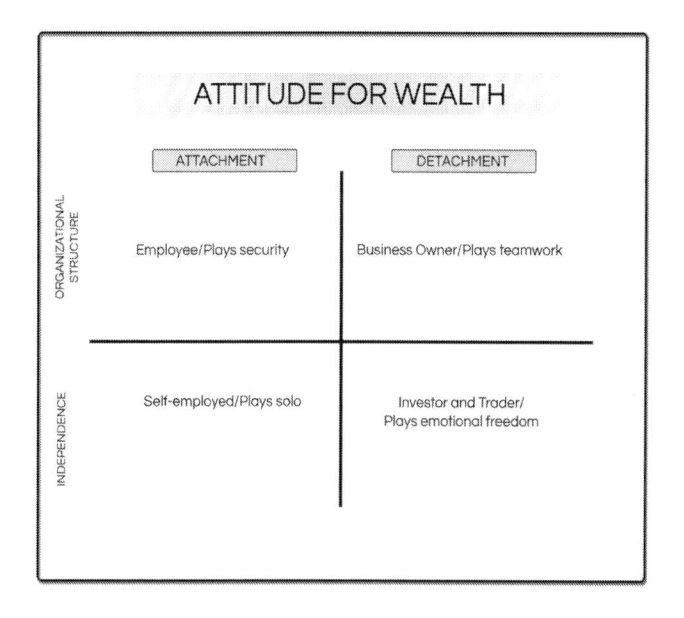

Figure 7: Attitude for Wealth

These four quadrants represent four groups of people and their attitudes toward wealth. The first-quadrant people manifest attachment security of an organizational structure. These are the people who remain employees for the rest of their lives, because they are afraid to leave their comfort zones, hence playing in security. The second-quadrant self-employed person is also attached to material wealth, but he seeks independence from the confinement of a 9-to-5 job. He plays solo. The third-quadrant business owner is detached from material wealth, but he still wants structure for his life. The fourth-quadrant investor/trader is emotionally free and maximizes on his independence. He is independent and detached from material wealth. By investor/trader, we don't mean someone who works with stocks; any one can be an investor/trader as long as he is willing to invest in himself and to trade his talents and abilities for wealth. He is one who lives in emotional freedom and financial abundance.

All-In

The Ticket to Life is a process; it's a journey in a natural transformational step-by-step approach. This journey does not have shortcuts; each stop along the way and every step you take will bring you closer to emotional freedom. Financial freedom comes as a result of a new attitude toward wealth.

In *All-In*, every transformation comes with a price tag. When you get out of the rat race, you must decide to stay out. But staying out should not be partial. It's like getting board a train, in which you cannot board only half of your body. You need to get your whole self on-board or you will be left behind. Of course, you can't be 80% committed to this journey, but that would create false hope. You will only go back to holding onto the mask that you have taken off.

In this case, complete detachment is important. It is only by completely detaching yourself from external things can you have control over your emotions and life.

When you dive into a pool, you need to dive with your whole body. Your hands and feet can't stay behind. Your whole body must take the leap, and become submerged.

In the complete submersion when you can no longer feel the ground beneath your feet, you will be able to apply the theory of swimming to the practice of swimming and find that you can do it. It cannot happen apart from that. You can *think* about how to swim. You can understand the techniques and movements. But until you actually take that plunge, you will never truly *know*.

Indeed, buying this Ticket to Life means you must make the decision to board the train. But don't leave an escape route—lock all the doors behind you so you will never go back.

The Power of 1%

What happens if you don't go all in? A man found himself in a dire financial situation, so he had to sell his home. His friend said, "Let me buy your house so you can have the money you need. When you get back on your feet, I promise to sell the house back to you." Assured that he would get his house back, the man agreed in one condition—that he would sell his house and everything in it except for a nail on the wall near the front door. He told his friend he wanted to remain as the rightful owner of this nail. His friend agreed, thinking, "It's only a tiny nail. I have the whole house."

After a couple of years, the man finally made enough money to buy his house back. However, his friend had backed out on his word and didn't want to sell back the house. The man lost his house and everything in it, except for the nail in the wall near the front door.

From time to time, he would come and hang things on the nail. The first thing he hung was an old painting. His friend thought nothing of it. It was just an old painting. The next thing he hung was a jacket. His friend thought it was odd, but he couldn't do anything about it because the nail rightfully belonged to the original owner of the house. Then one night, the man came and hung a dead dog on the nail.

His friend protested, saying, "You can't leave that here!" The original owner said, "Why not, it's my nail, so I'll hang whatever I want on that nail." His friend couldn't complain; however, the dead dog stunk up the whole house and he had no choice but to sell it back to the original owner.

Come to think of it, it was a small nail that made up less than one percent of the house. But because his friend didn't have ownership of 100 percent of the house, the original homeowner was able to take the house back. The point of the story is this: if you fail to detach yourself completely from external things, you will only end up going back where you started. You continue living in the old ways and operating under the same limiting beliefs.

Be the Author of Your Joy

Once you have detached yourself from external factors, you will then declare yourself as the author of your joy, which is an emotion that starts within. Joy results from the fulfillment of your purpose in life.

Most people immerse themselves in busyness rather than significance, never realizing that all efforts pertaining to wealth will only leave them unsatisfied, empty, and frustrated. In their kind of life, they watch the clock, count every second as time passes, and think about how much longer they can take it.

On the contrary, when you live your passion, time flies. It's like everything has a natural flow to it and you experience freedom, simply because you have aligned your work with your purpose. To be the author of your joy, you need to know your master plan. You need to know where you're going to direct your decisions and actions toward achieving your joy.

Happiness without a Reason

Deepak Chopra once said that if you were happy for a particular reason, the fear of losing that reason would constantly surround you. This means that detachment is critical for your happiness so that nothing—and no one—can control your emotions but you.

The quality of your life will grow by increasing degrees as you learn to maintain your own happiness apart from circumstances.

The subconscious mind cannot differentiate between the words you speak, the emotions you feel and the thoughts you dwell upon. So the moment you feel just a smidge better, you will enjoy a higher quality of life. Focusing on positive inner pictures, words and senses will cause the subconscious to start believing this is real and transform them into your real-life experiences.

Position of Entitlement vs. Position of Gratitude

We often pursue material things because we want to project a certain "appearance". But this desire to appear better than others comes from a place of pride. By now, you must understand that living truly requires letting go of the image you want to portray. In that way, you can become authentically yourself. Aside from that, it is not proper to compare ourselves with others since we take on different journeys.

Part of the process of detaching yourself from the wrong sources of happiness is humility. People tend to feel they are entitled to certain things by putting on masks to appear worthy or better than others. Others believe they're entitled to wealth because they work hard day in and day out, while some feel they deserve the best jobs because they studied in the best schools. A few others think they should be in great relationships because they work hard to look good physically.

The pride and desperation that come with thoughts of entitlements make us operate in anxiety and frustration. Moreover, these allow us to resent because they are not what we are aiming for, to begin with. The negativity and ungratefulness inherent in us increase as they go out, eventually boomeranging back to us a monster of a consequence.

Playing Small

Playing small may have been your default way of living. This has kept you running in the rat race and staying within the bounds of mediocrity. You have focused on things that limit you that you become easily magnified since they appear far more powerful than they are in reality. Then you cower in fear and get enslaved by circumstance. Playing small will keep you blaming other people for those unwanted things. Because you play small, you cannot reason out that your destructive behaviors result from other people's behavior or your reaction to the situation.

Playing Big

In contrast, playing big is about committing yourself to bringing about transformation in your life. It's an all-or-nothing deal. It's about buying your Ticket to Life and boarding the train to get to the promised destination, which is a more abundant life.

Playing big also means committing yourself to following your joy and deciding to become a better you. It's about being present in your life, instead of operating on autopilot all the time. Needless to say, when you're present and committed, gratitude and joy naturally follow.

Playing big is about treating life with gratitude rather than entitlement. Instead of focusing on what other people didn't do for you or how horrible a situation is for you, you should be grateful for the people around you and the great things that happen to you. Playing big is being grateful for your blessing.

Playing big is no longer about what you *have*; it's about looking at what you can *give*, what you can contribute to the world as a part of your purpose in life. When you play big, you don't spend your time complaining about bad relationships, horrible job, or depressing life. You must see those breakdowns as opportunities to create something new and renew your commitment to living out your purpose in life. You need to view them as a way to experience how things are working out in your life in a much bigger way than you can ever comprehend.

Be a Farmer

To follow through with your decision to follow your joy, take a lesson from the farmer. If you look at the farmer's life and routine, you will recognize important and practical principles to guide you in discovering and cultivating your emotional freedom. The farmer follows a process and applies it daily to transform his endeavors into successes. By applying the lesson of the farmer in our own lives, we can transform our own experiences, feelings, attempts, and desires into successful lives.

Sowing and Reaping

Looking back at the farmer's story, the first thing we can observe about him is that he knows the concept of sowing and reaping. In relation to that, a Biblical verse presents a new way of considering the world. It reads, "Whoever sows sparingly will also reap sparingly, and whoever sows generously will also reap generously" (2 Corinthians 9:6, NIV). This principle differs from that which governs our living. In the slave mindset, if you lose money, you lose money. When you give money away, you decrease your net worth.

In contrast, the principle behind the Biblical verse suggests that you need to give up something to gain something better.

When you detach yourself from material things, and let go of what you currently have, you will gain back emotional freedom and financial abundance. You must give something of yourself in order to receive something of much greater worth.

Farmers understand that reaping a harvest entails investing in seeds. Without seeds, crops will never have a chance to grow and feed the populace. Similarly, freeing yourself of your materialistic desires and the masks you have held for the longest time translates to reaping a life of emotional freedom and financial abundance. But you cannot do so unless you are willing to invest your time, resources, and yourself to experience a bountiful harvest. You cannot expect something from nothing.

The Law of Deliberate Creation

Farmers operate under the Law of Deliberate Creation. This law states that wherever you place your attention, thoughts, imagination, beliefs and feelings, it is the same place where your harvest will come from. If you dwell in fear, you will also harvest fear. Farmers are focused on the harvest, not just planting the seed. They plow and nurture their land, and patiently wait for harvest—they know what is coming to them. When they plant potatoes, they know that potatoes—not melon—will grow and will be their harvest.

Therefore, you must plant the right seeds to harvest what you desire; you must also commit to protecting it so that weeds do not take over.

Like the farmer, you should also operate under the Law of Deliberate Creation. In alignment with the LOA, intentionality is the key to creating for your life. What is your purpose? What is your master plan? Envision your future and imagine what it's like to live out that master plan. Belief is a necessary element in the process: the more you focus on the master plan, the more you will manifest it into your reality.

You will certainly experience such showdowns, but cannot give up and get back to your old self. The farmer protects his investment; similarly, you must also commit yourself to seeing your master plan and living it out to experience true joy.

Operate in Faith

A farmer won't think, "Harvest time will never come." He is confident of the fact that when he sows, he will reap. He doesn't doubt the natural order, and plans his life around the harvest. He has deliberately created it in his mind before it ever physically was.

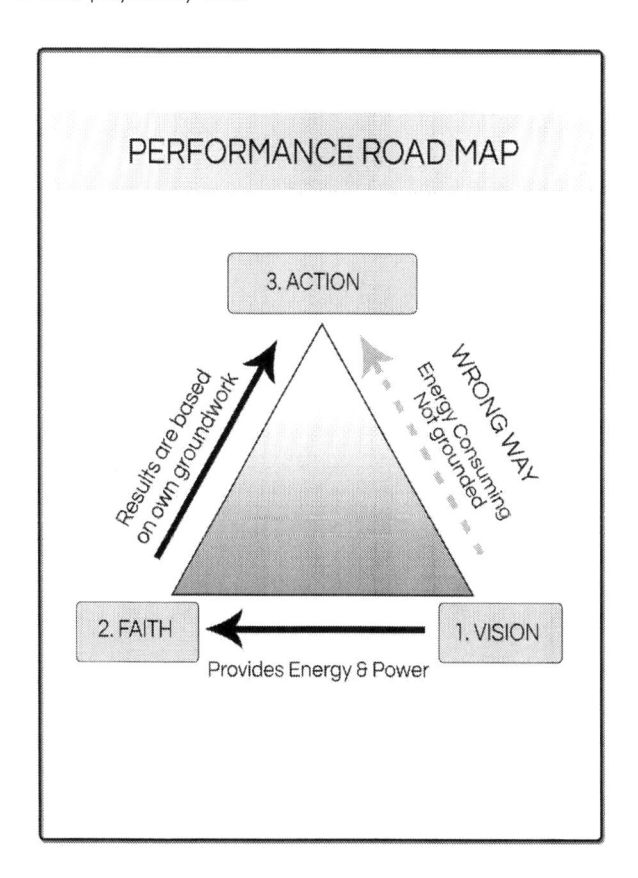

Figure 8: Performance Road Map

Many people have a vision in life, but they go from vision to action without waiting for the right time or going through the process. They miss out an important step in performance that involves faith. When they move from action to faith their energy is drained because they're relying on themselves. They take shortcuts and perform without any help from a higher power. However, when people base their actions on their vision and on faith, the outcomes of their action will be powerful and well grounded.

Faith plays a big role in knowing what will be. You can invest your resources on your master plan and let go of the things that have kept you back, because you *know* that what you sow, so shall you reap. That's the natural order of things. You can't think, "Maybe my dreams are just too big and too impossible."

Develop Patience

We can also learn from the farmer's story the value of patience. The farmer doesn't expect to reap the harvest overnight, in the same week or month. It takes time and patience. As crops do not grow out of season, he cannot try to harvest them early in hope that they have already born some fruit. If he does that, the crops would die.

In the same way, we cannot expect that detaching ourselves from materialistic desires today will result in emotional freedom tomorrow. We need to understand that patience is part of the process. We need to direct our behaviors, thoughts, and actions towards preparing for this "harvest" to come the way farmers do

A lot of people do not understand the concept of waiting. That's because we live in a fast-paced world with everyone getting everything in the most convenient manner. We have microwaveable food; we have instant messaging, and no-strings-attached relationships. We've been used to immediate gratification and don't have the patience to *be* patient. But this fastness will not work for us. To enjoy the harvest, we will need to wait patiently for our master plan to unfold.

What Season Are You In?

Farmers know how to read the seasons. They know when it's time to sow, and when to reap. They also know which crops to plant during a particular season, so their efforts will not be wasted. They won't eat their *seeds* because they understand that it's a time of sowing for something better. When the season of reaping comes, they will be able to enjoy the harvest.

Just like the farmer, you also need to recognize the season you're in. Is it of sowing? Of waiting and preparing? Or is it of reaping? Understanding the season you are in allows you to think, decide, and behave accordingly. It may be the season to let go of whatever is trying to limit you from being the real you (like a limiting belief or an attachment to material wealth). It may be the season to invest your time, energy, or money, and finally sow the seeds for your future.

Within the period of sowing, you must avoid eating your seeds. In a bigger context, it means that you should avoid putting all your money into buying a luxury car or a large house. Instead, use it productively, so you can reap a favorable harvest. If you eat your seed right now, what harvest will you be able to produce?

For example, to become a world-class musician, you must invest your time in honing your skill. To leave a legacy of being a humanitarian, you must volunteer for the causes you believe in. To become a successful entrepreneur, you must invest in your own business. Therefore, if you want to be emotionally free and financially successful, you must invest in a life coach. I believe that people who invest in their well-being are ultimately the ones who will be successful in life.

The difference between emotionally wealthy and emotionally poor people is that the latter work to earn, while the former work to learn. The wealthy invest in coaches so they can have the best quality of life possible. They seek emotional freedom, rather than material wealth. This kind of attitude and mindset makes them successful. The blueprint they have geared towards having an emotionally free life makes them wealthy rather than the money they have in the bank.

Are you in a place of waiting for your harvest to come? Are you preparing for this master plan to unfold? That means you've already brought the masks down and let go of the many important things that brought you superficial joy. Now, it may be quiet, but don't question the silence, although it's not easy to wait for something. However, the quiet times are the best so you can prepare yourself. Are you ready to receive the harvest you desire? A lot of people pray to win the lottery, but they have not planned what they'd do with all that money.

Now you must build on the skills you have and become more emotionally aware. Now you must grow your commitment and faith to see your master plan through to completion. As you wait for your breakthroughs, you should prepare for their coming, but while waiting, you can focus on building your master plan. It doesn't end with one breakthrough though; you prepare for another, and continue to do so throughout life.

Are you in a time of reaping? This is the season for enjoying the benefits of your sowing. You have invested your resources and committed yourself to protecting your investment. The patience and diligence have paid off as you experience the joys of the harvest in the physical realm. Apparently, it's no longer a picture in your mind; it's the actualization of the episodes you included in your life script.

As you enjoy this time with gratitude and humility, plan your next steps and prepare for the next season, which may nearly be upon you again. Prepare for bigger breakthroughs and set aside the seed from the harvest and the possibility of investing once again, so you can create a cycle of abundance.

If thoughts, beliefs and emotions create life experiences, you must choose how you will respond to each season. You can choose to create instead of reacting by default. When you react, you subconsciously create the things that you do *not* desire for yourself, and move into a position of powerlessness. However, once you deliberately create joy and abundance, you'll be able to create one breakthrough after another as you bring your master plan into reality.

The Butterfly Experience

Real transformation comes through a natural process. This process refers to the development of consciousness similar to what the caterpillar goes through in order to become a butterfly. It cannot be forced into it becoming a butterfly. While in the cocoon, the caterpillar is at the standstill, patiently enduring until it's time to break free as a butterfly.

Symbolically, the season of the cocoon represents the season of waiting. In your case, the season of waiting may be the most awkward phase in your development because there seems to be no progress. But though it may not be visible to the naked eye, a metamorphosis is underway.

Surrender must happen before you can move on to the next phase of transformation into a butterfly. Your own season of waiting is similar to the cocoon; it may be increasingly difficult to maintain faith because you cannot see any part of your life script in your reality. But this is the time to be humble and patient. Nature will always take its course.

Letting go of the need to try to force things to happen and imagining the good that will come with an improved mindset and emotions mean that the experience that you have longed for will come at the right time. While waiting, all doors of the past are closed so complete transformation may take place.

The caterpillar-to-butterfly experience illustrates that the process of change does not have shortcuts. When you follow your joy in life, you cannot skip steps along the way, which may involve solitude, loneliness, and waiting. This convenience-driven society may fool you into operating and thinking that shortcuts are viable options. To be emotionally free and financially abundant, you will undergo trying processes, because each step aims to develop your strength and resolve. You must remember that joy often comes through hardship.

Before you can dive, you need to learn to swim

One of the most challenging things I experienced in this journey was going all-in, which is the most important part of the process. It is similar to diving, which entails complete submersion. You need to learn how to swim before you can dive. If you can't swim, you won't be able to dive because you will drown. In like manner, you will not be able to let go of everything and go all in if you aren't prepared to do so. That's because you'll tend to leave doors open so you can come back.

When you learn to swim, you prepare yourself to set off on the journey. The first step is to begin with an end in mind. As I left for Canada, I was already thinking of the end I wanted. But I was not going to come back until I was the better version of myself. I wasn't going to come back unless I found myself. At that stage in my life, I already had an end in mind. I was resolved to going back knowing the secret to my life's happiness.

Learning the Ropes

Once you have defined your end point, find a mentor. Life is better when you have someone else to teach you to get through it successfully. The truth is that not everyone is fit for this task. However, he must not be just that someone you need—he has to be someone who has successfully done what you want to do in your own life. This is what I've seen time and time again with my clients. It's a worthy investment to hire a life coach because you need someone who'll mentor you through this process. It's a priceless investment to work with someone who's been there because he has had experience in helping people find the quality of life they've always wanted.

Facing the Facts

The third step is the process of lowering the mask and losing the fear. Doing so requires you honesty about who you really are. You may have had life experiences that you aren't proud of, but you should not be afraid of your past. If you are honest, you become vulnerable, which is a beautiful feeling. You need to be open to prepare yourself to go all-in and experience a life of transformation.

In 2010, I was interviewed for an article about my life journey. I openly shared the fears and weaknesses I had back then. In this interview, I lowered my mask publicly. Everybody who never knew me suddenly knew more than they perhaps ever wanted to know. They knew that I was just like them. I related to them my experiences with fears. I also said that through the hard work of coming to know myself, I also experienced joy like never before.

In that interview, I thought it was important to say that weights had been lifted and that I freed myself from any pretension or illusion. I expected different people would have different reactions to that interview, but I knew that I was on the way to being fully emotionally free. Honestly, it really didn't matter what other people thought about me. I was only being honest. Being honest led me to realizing that I had gone all-in, announced it to the world, and more importantly conquered my fears.

Dwelling on Joy

When we dwell on the idea of joy and the possibility of having it, we operate under hope and expectancy. We believe we will receive it, and this belief produces limitless joy. If you're unable to give it all, you may not be ready but that's okay. However, there will come a time when you need to decide to go all-in to be truly happy.

It's all or nothing. When the time comes and you dive in, you need to close every door behind you. There's no turning back. This was the decision I made years ago, and I have never regretted it since.

MENTOR'S SECTION: DR. JUDITH ORLOFF

Dr. Judith Orloff, healer and author of The Ecstasy of Surrender, played an important role in transforming the face of psychiatry. She taught me how your intuition and spirituality can actually affect your physical health. She suggests that we play the role of the keeper of innate intuitive intelligence, which should be perceptive enough to give us the power to heal and prevent our own illness. Traditional healthcare usually disregards any therapeutic power related with intuition and spirituality. Dr. Orloff advocated democracy of healing, wherein every aspect of our being is granted a vote for achieving total health.

In addition, Dr. Orloff also tells us that it is our birthright, as healthcare providers and recipients, to reclaim the power of intuition to build energy and well-being.

In her book, she describes the power of letting go our everyday life. She describes this as a sane and enlivened alternative to pushing, forcing, and over-controlling people and situations. She also shares her showdowns and the realization to embrace her gift of intuition.

> **"I'm intrigued with the idea of surrender not as defeat or loss, as it is frequently thought of, but as a positive, intuitive way of living, a power that grows as you develop trust in the moment as well as in change and the unknown. Contrary to common stereotypes that equate surrender with weakness, I'm presenting it as a way to gain mastery of your life, not give up power."**
>
> **- Judith Orloff**

MENTOR'S SECTION: ASTRONAUT EDGAR MITCHELL

Edgar Mitchell is regarded as the sixth man on the moon. Mitchell explored the Fra Mauro region for two days, a territory that Apollo 13 never reached. He was a Navy officer before joining NASA. He retired from both institutions to pursue his passion for understanding the nature of human consciousness. Because of his exposure to space travel, he became more aware of the connections between humans.

When the Sputnik went up, he directed his career toward going to space one day. It took him nine years, additional flight experience, additional jet hours, space management experience, and working at the U.S. Air Force Aerospace Research Pilot School. He was selected in April 1966 to serve in backup assignments before getting a flight himself. He backed up the Apollo 10, the first mission to fly the type of spacecraft near the moon.

Mitchell was supposed to be the lunar module pilot for Apollo 13, along with Alan Shepard. However, as training progressed, Shepard chose to take more time and to move the trip back a flight to Apollo 14. Apollo 13 ended up being a near-disaster when an oxygen tank ruptured in space. Before Apollo 14 left the ground, additional safety measures and procedures were set in place. In 1971, Apollo 14 lifted off and yielded 100 pounds of rock for scientists on earth.

Mitchell returned from the moon a changed man. He gained a greater awareness of the forces that shape the universe. He experienced the sensation of "a sense of universal connectedness" from having experienced being between two worlds. Mitchell founded the Institute of Noetic Sciences in the 1970s to explore what consciousness is and how it relates to cosmology and causality.

"There is an information flow in our bodies . . . Our intuitive information is really of a quantum nature . . . what we call our intuition is our sixth sense when in reality it should be called our first sense."

- Edgar Mitchell

Chapter 7
Forgive the Past

The only journey is the one within.

– Rainer Maria Rilke

The need to cut ties

Before you can move forward, you must be sure nothing is holding you back. Imagine a bird tied down to the ground. It won't be able to fly away as long as it's tied down. Only if it is able to cut himself loose can it get anywhere. In like manner, this is why a mentor is a very important part of the process. Mentors can help you cut through the fears that have tied you to the ground so that you can soar. Be ready to let go of people who do not support your inner growth.

> **TRANSFORMATION PRINCIPLE 10:**
>
> ***Be ready to let go of people who do not support your inner growth***

Forgiveness is part of your journey. If you cannot forgive those who have hurt you in the past, you will forever be connected to the person or circumstance. If you don't forgive, you will always be connected to them. Time heals all wounds, they say, but time does nothing in the healing if forgiveness is pending. Withholding forgiveness gives power to the person or situation that has hurt you to continue to haunt you for the rest of your life; to take control back, you must decide to forgive. It is the only way to cut the thread and be free.

Not forgiving those people who hurt you back then will only block your feelings. You will attract the feelings you hold against the person you refuse to forgive. At this point, I should remind you that the LOA reacts based on your feelings. It doesn't distinguish between feelings you desire and feelings you cannot control. It will simply deliver based on the feelings you harbor.

Shifting Gears

Shifting your life's gears requires forgiveness for past actions, whether they are your own or someone else's. Doing so may seem impossible, but you go through the process to experience emotional freedom.

This doesn't mean you have to trust that person again. Forgiveness is different from trust: while trust is your belief in a person's reliability, forgiveness is the act of getting rid of the need to avenge yourself. Only when you forgive will you start trusting in yourself and your own journey.

Nobody can turn back the time and make things "unhappen." You can only operate in the present. You have the choice. Either, you forgive and cancel the debt that the painful experience caused you. Or, you can hold these offenders in debt forever, with the promise to get them back for what they did.

The illusion comes in when you imagine that you will be the winner if you can exact revenge on them. But the desire to punish another person creates negative emotions in you, which, when they well up, return to you with boomerang force. Without realizing it, you have "ordered" whatever you were feeling to manifest into reality; the LOA always aims to deliver the thing you asked for.

> **TRANSFORMATION PRINCIPLE 11:**
>
> **Without realizing it, you have "ordered" whatever you were feeling to manifest into reality; the LOA always aims to deliver the thing you asked for.**

I don't believe in coincidence. I believe that everything is a product of the LOA working out reality. Every experience is an opportunity for learning. Some attribute the opportunities that come to them to a higher power, but all people are responsible for their own feelings. Considering what I am trying to do to your life, I can only lead you to the practical knowledge, but I cannot think for you.

We are actually the causes of our own circumstances. Once we determine the cause of the negative circumstances we are in, we can overwrite our blueprints to shift the conditions in our lives. Shifting your emotional state from negative to positive state will allow you to begin forgiving those who have hurt you.

Journey to my roots

Take time to figure out where your own roots are and where you are coming from in life. If you remain unaware of your roots, you cannot live a full life. You will never understand what a fully free and full life can be. Since your roots are an important part of you, you should discover this deep inner part of yourself. Doing so will help you gain freedom from yourself.

If you never knew your birth parents or siblings growing up, perhaps now is the time to begin the journey toward a healing. Discover your real roots and find out where you came from. When you understand where you came from, the power to build on your master plan with a much clearer and solid perspective becomes more feasible.

Knowing your roots can be quite nerve-wracking. In fact, many people grow up without knowledge of their background. They grow up never knowing their biological parents. Some know their biological parents, but they might be relationally dysfunctional and so do not really know one another. It's completely common for people to live life disconnected from their past. Many people can probably relate far too easily to growing up with an incomplete sense of self because their parents weren't present physically or emotionally during their growing years. That was part of my story. I grew up without knowing my biological father.

Forgiving my roots

Without my biological father, I felt like there was a part of me that was always missing. To grow up holistically, a child must be connected to both his or her father and the mother's love. I have great respect for stepmothers, stepfathers and adoptive parents. But I am also completely in favor of a child or grown child knowing where he or she came from. My own stepfather knew the value of this and helped me in that journey. But growing up without my biological father, I did not feel the full source and strength of masculinity in my life. His absence affected me as though there was a massive void that I had to fill with my own Ego. As I came to understand the power that the Ego held over me to keep me in emotional bondage, I came to terms with my father's death, and forgave him for not being present. I realized too that death is not an excuse or a hindrance to forgiving someone. After all, forgiveness is not a physical issue, but a heart issue. It's an emotional feat, since you have to deal with your deep emotions when you forgive. There is no such thing as intellectual forgiveness.

Reconnecting

A boy needs his father to be able to fully establish his manhood. When I forgave my father, I was able to connect with my roots and establish my manhood through the force of freedom, which seemed to have been bestowed upon me by him even from afar. Forgiving my father created this connection between my father and me—a connection that not even death can undo.

When I forgave him, my feelings changed from, "Why did you leave me?" to "I'm very thankful I'm here, and it's because of you." The emotions I had harbored shifted from resentment to forgiveness, gratitude, and love.

Open your heart

How you respond to someone is completely up to you. Never think that you need to receive love from someone to give love in return. The greatest love comes when you don't want or deserve it. This is a test of your own emotional capacity to break free from the bonds so you will be taken into a bigger and better reality where love is not dependent on any one thing or circumstance but simply on your *being*.

Later in that journey, I discovered that others do not have the responsibility to make me feel loved. I had to open my heart to love—first loving myself so I could love others more. In my attempt to love myself, I also had to accept myself for who I really was behind the mask.

Have you ever decided to love your parents, your spouse, our children? Now I want to tell you this: make time to *be* with your loved ones, make time to get to know them and cherish them for who they are. Break free from your unforgiving state that might have dictated your past with them. Loving them even when they don't seem to deserve your love is actually your choice. Hold every moment that you have with them closely, because someday they will be gone. You can't take them back. Life is too short to live and dwell in being unforgiving. Love is not intellectual or explainable. It just is.

Forgiveness frees us from limiting beliefs

Broken trust. Abuse. Abandonment. These negative feelings result from harboring resentment toward someone who hurt us. Forgiving the people who might have caused you these negative feelings and other traumas will allow you to take back your power over yourself. Forgiving them means that you are worthy of the dignity and respect that you did not receive in the past.

Additionally, forgiving them will allow you to reclaim your lost power by breaking the emotional chains that have fettered you all these years. Other times, we cannot easily pinpoint the inflictor of the pain, but even the undefined needs to be forgiven. Indeed, it's vital to relinquish all negative thoughts toward yourself to allow yourself to experience ultimate freedom.

We all have something or someone in the past that we need to forgive. Often, they are authority figures that instilled in us unsupportive beliefs. They could be our parents who imparted illusions about life that have enslaved us to circumstance and masked people.

Sometimes—though it might be difficult to admit—we resent our parents for the not-so-obvious 'offense' of being overprotective and overly caring. Though their intentions were good, the same intentions caused us to learn a dependency on others. This dependency has translated into how we view life and ourselves, only in relation to others. This same dependency may have made it difficult for us to handle reality and survive. Well, this is one way the mask comes up. In your case, did your parents shelter you or give you room and encouragement to be your own person?

In some cases, authority figures may have encouraged you to aim for good grades in school, to pursue higher education, to work hard, to get a secure job and to climb the ladder of success. While these aren't bad the reasons *why* you chase after these things can be destructive and disempowering. As Robert Kiyosaki of *Rich Dad, Poor Dad* puts it, "Who controls the past controls the future, who controls the present controls the past."

When you let go of the past, you can create your better future; otherwise, you will remain a victim of your bad experiences with people, eventually trapping you in limiting beliefs. As you forgive the sources of limiting beliefs in your life, you can uncover the freedom to let go of those beliefs again and again. You can see offense, you can forgive offense, and you can move past offense.

The Life Sentence

Any deep-seated limiting beliefs serve as captors that take you as an emotional prisoner. When you refuse to forgive, you place yourself in a life sentence, and you are the only person who can set yourself free.

Furthermore, you may have placed limitations upon yourself or have faced disappointments, but what did you do next? What did you decide to do to survive situations like these in the future?

The thing is that we tend to deal with these limitations or setbacks by turning inward, from where we are never able to get out again. We lock ourselves into a detrimental cycle of viewing the world. When we set the negative thoughts and limitations, we place ourselves on trial and act as judge and jury. By this kind of action, we often convict ourselves more harshly than anyone would in the real world. Whenever life fails to go as planned, we set the verdict as "guilty".

Reversing the Life Sentence

Your mask may hide your perceived guilt from the world and may allow the world to see you as the person you wish you were. Take off the mask and *pretend* the past didn't happen. Be real. Be honest. Be vulnerable. Be willing to admit you were hurt. Then be willing to pick up the pieces, to forgive, and to move on.

Don't let the hurt control you or hide the real you anymore. Then shift the negativity toward new and positive emotions. Let the past become the past and no longer your present reality. In this way, you can become the Court of Appeals, and reverse the life sentences you've given. Afterwards, release yourself from the prison of unforgiveness you've placed yourself into.

Instead of allowing the past to imprison you, develop compassion for yourself. It is only when you've built a complete case to present to the Court of Appeals that old evidence can be thrown out. The Court of Appeals must hear the new case, so you must gather the courage to search within your heart for the people or circumstances you cannot forgive. When you're able to do this, turn your life sentence around.

One of the major problems with unforgiveness is that we're not even aware that a trial has taken place. We simply move on with our lives, oblivious to the walls we have put up, though we keep hitting the walls every day thinking this is just life. Overturning the life sentence is an important process to overwrite your blueprint. When there is unforgiveness, you will not be able to operate in abundance. When you are able to forgive the past, you can then renew the blueprint that has been dictating your life.

Healing

Forgiveness is critical to your journey because it involves healing your feelings. Without healing, living an emotionally free life would be impossible.

But before you can heal, your wounds need to be reopened, which will be a very painful process. But every tear, every regret, every fear, every pain and every stain is worth it. During the healing process, you will find yourself vulnerable; but no one has ever experienced healing by holding on to his or her sickness.

Three Emotional States

I started my journey in emotional brokenness, and then moved toward emotional healing to emotional freedom. My life's purpose now includes helping others experience their own emotional freedom. In this section, I will discuss the three emotional states. In which group do you belong, and are you content to stay there? Let's find out.

First State: Wearing the Mask to Please Others

The first emotional state is the one people find himself or herself in as they stay in the rat race of life. This state results from being in an environment that produces stagnation, and the people who are in this state have low self-esteem and self-respect. They sink into a state of depression in a way that they no longer care for their own bodies and just doing the same routine every day. These are the people who are *trying* to live rather than just living. But they have the power to set themselves free.

Second State: Waiting for Somebody Else's Help

The second emotional state is when people are at a standstill, because they silently drown themselves in their negative emotions, hence depleting their will to live. Depression may set in, and financial losses may hit hard. The longer someone stays in this state, the harder it is to get out. So where can you go from here? If you are at the breaking point, will you surrender everything and take the leap toward healing and emotional freedom, or will you give up?

Third State: Moving Forward Without Fear

In this emotional state, energy and power are regained. One who is in this state begins to see the difference between self-esteem and intellectual knowledge. However, this form of intellect does not create happiness, satisfaction, or wealth. If you are in this state, you can detach yourself from the world and become the master of your emotions. You will start to feel instantly lighter and more positive toward life as you begin to appreciate your life. Hope is resurrected and you can move towards uncovering your purpose in life and living in it with unexplainable joy.

How a Life-Guide Can Help

No one can do CPR by himself or herself; somebody else has to do the resuscitation on you. This person can help bring you back to consciousness when you are emotionally broken. In my journey, I sought help from several mentors to find emotional healing. Now I would like to return the favor by helping people walk their own journey to freedom. I know I can do this because I have been there. I like to call such a person a Life-Guide. A Life-Guide, before he performs his task, needs to be able to be a role model for others. Life performance guidance addresses life transformations that bring emotional freedom and inner peace and abundance on a relational, financial, physical and spiritual level.

Most people fail to recognize the role of faith in their emotional journey. I tell you, without the conscious decision to trust a power outside of yourself, reach real inner peace within you will be impossible. Faith enables you to live in the now. In my case, faith generated the feelings of being an emotional multimillionaire, eventually leading to financial harvest. When the transformation is complete, you will never look at finances in the same way. Money will be reaching to you to help you fulfill your real purpose in life and to be invested for your growth and development.

Now, I see myself as an entrepreneur whose goal is to help you live a full life. The logo that represents my V.I.P. Coaching Services is that of a money tree. I call it 'V.I.P.' because I consider each person a Very Important Person. If you are already a V.I.P. but only by the estimation of others, you might need a transformation to see yourself as what you are—that you're also a V.I.P. According to Chinese legend, the money tree, a symbol of affluence and nobility, is so holy that it can bring wealth to people who plant and nurture it.

Our V.I.P. services help and guide clients to plant seeds to enable them to develop an abundant harvest in all aspects of life. Transforming your blueprint is like re-planting a tree. As you plant your tree, you can plant with seeds of positive emotions that will grow roots based on real-life purpose and consequently develop the best kind of harvest.

Leadership and Forgiveness

Leadership is a two-edged sword. Some transformed leaders take responsibility for their lives and set themselves up as role models for others. But too many leaders act like paid mercenaries. The world needs more transformed leaders with integrity and honesty toward seeking, knowing, and living their own life purposes. You can only become a true leader and mentor when you forgive your past and take a close inner look at your own life.

A real leader brings people from one point to another, even at the expense of his life. He takes charge of his life, leading both intellectually and emotionally. This leader knows that emotional states always impact the way one leads, whether in a company, family, or social group.

The Sick Monetary System

Working as a trader and banker for so many years, I saw the inner workings of the monetary system; I also saw how closely it relates to the state of our own emotions and mind. The current monetary and banking system does not serve the inner growth and development of a person, just as your old way of thinking has been preventing you from moving past your hard times.

Banks have specific purposes for which they are useful, like providing mortgage financing and investment banking. Analogously, you can also see a kind of brokenness we need to deal with on a personal emotional level. Our masks once had a purpose as well—to allow us to feel okay. But when you decided to move past "okay" to "alive and free", the purpose of the mask is defeated.

My research on banking history brought me to a startling halt when I came to see a connection between the banking system and the behaviors of people within the rat race. The monetary system is sick, and seems to be getting sicker daily. It seems there is a covert conspiracy being played out by the few who run the banking system to keep people running in the rat race. That they do so that they can never find complete satisfaction and will forever be striving for more and more money, but never attain it because the money they work so hard for is, in fact, an illusion in itself.

The common system that most of the world uses these days is called Fractional Reserve Banking, which is a practice of generating an overabundance of money without having the value to back it up. With an increasing world population, more money is constantly being put in circulation. But paper money essentially has no more value today than the paper on which it's printed. The small group that controls this system essentially places the world in bondage—people work longer hours to make more money with less value. They give up themselves for a piece of paper, and lose the valuable commodity of time and ability for self-reflection.

By valuing money, people succeed in increasing the value of the material world. That is because those in the rat race are as unhealthy as the banking system; they also constantly believe they need more to find happiness and success. At this point may I remind you that when you take off the mask, step out of the rat race, and reevaluate your view of yourself and the financial world, the link suddenly becomes apparent. You can also see how the financial system has essentially been playing you, molding you into the perfect consumer—unhappy, unfulfilled, full of negative emotions, and searching for a deeper joy.

As I said, this was the conclusion I had come to when I considered my emotional well-being. However, I urge you put some thought and time into seeking out the correlation between the financial system and yourself. The monetary system is sick and needs healing, but it can only be healed if people recognize the need to heal it. Analogously, your inner self and emotions will only be healed if you see the need.

When you see the illness of the system, you can disconnect from it to avoid being infected any longer by its brokenness. The Bible states that you cannot serve two masters at the same time. You cannot be a slave of this system and be the master of your own life. When you successfully change your view of the monetary system on which the world is built, your blueprint will change as well.

Currently, we need a new monetary system to serve all people in a healthy way, just as we all need a new blueprint to serve each of us in the healthy way that emotional freedom requires.

Breaking the Ties That Bind

Growing into your master plan takes time; it begins with realization of the sickness of the old system; disillusionment progresses into desire, and desire gives birth to change. You won't experience your new life under the master plan all at once. It unfolds in parts, and you will discover each new part at exactly the right time and in the right order. Let go of the old and welcome the new.

Learn to use your newfound power of forgiveness to break the bonds of the old. Make daily use of the knowledge you've gained, and as you do, you will see your life sentence lift, your source of sickness removed, and the truth behind the current monetary system revealed. All your limiting beliefs will begin to show themselves for what they are—lies—and you will finally experience your truer and more powerful blueprint.

MENTOR'S SECTION: ELIZABETH CLARE PROPHET

Elizabeth Clare Prophet was a longtime spiritual leader of the Church Universal and Triumphant. She came to Montana after the death of her second husband, Mark Prophet, who founded the Church Universal and Triumphant, under its original name, the Summit Lighthouse. Their church believed in the science of the spoken word.

Prophet's church received media attention in 1988, when a 16000-acre fire was spreading outward Yellowstone National Park. There were about 250 members of the congregation who gathered in the meadow to pray and to deliver decrees. Members, with outstretched arms chanted, "Reverse the tide, roll them back, and set all free." The fire stopped at the church border. The slurry bombers stopped the blaze, but Prophet and the church believed it was the power of the spoken prayer that protected them.

> "I find that God by any name can be reduced to this sense of the eternal Presence. It defines being, and I see it as a sphere of intense light that marks the point of my origin. It is the permanent part of me, of which I am very aware, and the point to which I will return at the conclusion of this life."
>
> **- Elizabeth Claire Prophet**

HEALER'S SECTION: MARGRIT BERISH

Margrit Berish, medium, therapeutic card reader, and healer, grew up with six siblings in the Swiss region of Emmental. She's always been clairvoyant and felt keen sense, without realizing how this made her unique. All along, her talents aligned with her master plan, which is to be a healer for people who'd need her gifts in order to experience emotional and spiritual freedom.

On a personal note, Berish helped me uncover the emotional bondages that I call decrees. My experience with her is an essential part of my emotional journey because it opened me up to seeing my purpose in life and enjoying inner peace. I realized that unresolved decrees could hold you back from being happy and free. Healing of hurt feelings is the key to living in abundance.

In the past, people came to Berish to consult their concerns with relationships. However, there's a changing pattern in the present as people are more concerned about karma or decrees. They want to know why there are strong suits or strongholds in their lives. In the present, people come to her for healing so they won't be able to pass their emotional troubles to their children.

Berish has a gift through which, she can access information that guides her clients to uncover forgotten or repressed memories. She is able to see their energies as misdirected and identify fractures in their lives, such as taboo family secrets, trauma, and unhappiness.

Today, Berish's services include counselling and coaching sessions. She organizes courses and leads healing sessions that include collaborations with medical healing. She is also the Co-Founder of the 'Verein der Begegnung' (Association of Encounter), which seeks to work on the 22 levels of consciousness in human development on one hand, and to form a platform where people with different interests can communicate their fields of knowledge.

Part III
Move Forward Without Looking Back

This quote from a workshop held by Esther Hicks more than a decade ago has always inspired me:

> When you are in sync with the Energy of Source, which is the Energy of Well-being, Well-being is your experience. And when you're not you don't feel so good. Everything that you're living is a perfect replica of the vibration of your being.

The power encompassed in how you feel is probably the most important message I can give to direct the Law of Attraction into your favor. In my coaching and workshops I help people get in touch with and express their feelings. We live in a generation where feelings are suppressed and talking about them is best left in the psychologist's office. By showing your feelings, you're able to provide facts. I want to share an example from the stock markets around the world and what really makes them move.

Feelings, Emotions, and Market Prices

Feelings and emotions control the rise and fall of market prices. Before any decision is made, feelings and emotions come into play. They are the roots of decision-making and provide the facts on which everything operates. The facts, for example, may include the price of equity. Since most of the participants in the stock market act through fear and greed, they will seldom make any profit because they do not act in faith that there will always be plenty, but that they only follow the law of supply and demand, trying to hoard whatever they can because they perceive it is lacking. The stockholders are victims of circumstance; similarly, I was also a victim in the beginning of my career. Is there a difference between feelings and emotions? In my own experience and transformation I realized that I obtained a better state just by using my life script as a guide for my heart and mind.

Visualizations are a great technique to feel better. Emotions are the driver coming out of a feeling. Emotions make you take action. Emotional freedom comes when you can act apart from fear or greed. This is action based on your life's purpose, and is neutral, meaning you are not valuing or judging the outside through emotions.

Once you attain emotional freedom, it is yours forever; it is sealed with a quality of life that stands apart from the general work-life balance. In the stock market, the emotional free traders or investors make the most profit. Winning traders and investors want to be right in a certain stock so they wouldn't follow the trends and simply act according to their self-set risk profile.

T. Harv Eker, author of *Secrets of a Millionaire Mind*, once told me "I'd rather be rich than right". So think twice about your buy-and-hold mutual fund or retirement account. Once liberated from negative thoughts and feelings, you will begin to enjoy synchronicity in your life. Many call this happy moment as "serendipity". Money and renewed cash flow will come when you least expect it.

Chapter 8
Practice Gratitude Now

Your attitude, not your aptitude, will determine your altitude.

Zig Ziglar

The Power of Humility

Have you ever considered this thought: *I should be rich right now because of the hard work I've been putting into this company* or *After all I've done for this company, I should be running this place by now?* Such statements of entitlement reveal a person who usually operates under negativity rather than positivity.

When I say humility, it does not mean being a doormat. It has nothing to do with buying the cheapest car because you don't want to be labeled as fancy or flashy. However, hiding yourself and appearing to be something you are not, is *not* humility. When you're doing something for the sake of what other people will think, even if you want to *appear* humble, is still a form of mask wearing and pride.

When you do that, your life's vitality will naturally be lessened. By being humble, like a beggar, you are willing to ask for help so you can move forward in life. Perhaps you have a university degree, money in the bank, intellectual knowledge, but if you can act in the vantage of a beggar in acknowledging that you need help, then you are already richer than the rest of the world.

Once you think that you don't need anyone in your life because you can do things on your own, you begin to work against yourself. Pride is bred when you attach your identity, happiness, or worth to the luxuries. Pride is dangerous and disempowering. It creates a sense of entitlement and brings with it hoards of negativity that will drown you. Once drowned, you won't be able to move forward in victory and success.

When we were young, we were conditioned to obtain good grades, get safe jobs, and make lots of money to buy "stuff" to make us happy for a short time. Humility is not naturally ingrained into our beings, growing up. As children, we were naturally brought up to associate our value with performance and material wealth.

If our value is related to performance and wealth, awareness for our weakness and limitations has been something we have avoided. True humility is linked to our journey of finding self-esteem and self-acceptance rooted in us. It allows us to expose our vulnerabilities with courage and peace, and to be okay with our weaknesses.

When you're in a position in which you can neither accept nor admit your weaknesses, then you remain stuck in them. Only when you are okay admitting your weaknesses can you ask other people for help and lift yourself up out of the mess of your past life.

When you realize that you don't need to go on this journey alone, you will experience a burden lifted from your chest, freeing you to overcome your weaknesses. You don't need to be frustrated by your limitations, instead acknowledge them since they are opportunities to muster up strength and courage to conquer them. When you feel like this, you will accomplish your goals.

However, you must learn to humble yourself by asking for help, to build connections. Your connections with humanity are more significant and beneficial than your attachment to material things. As you learn to show gratitude, you will learn to connect with people, and open yourself up to more good.

The Law of Vibration

The Law of Vibration, "Nothing rests; everything moves; everything vibrates." This means that the emotions and thoughts you have do not remain in your mind and in your heart. They move to your subconscious mind and manifest themselves into your reality.

Accordingly, gratitude acts as a turbo force in the manifestation process. It's only when you have genuine gratitude in your heart that you can truly manifest the things you want in your life. True gratitude includes forgiving every pain and regret but being thankful for them as they, too, have a purpose, from which a lesson needs to be learned.

We humans are made of moving matter. We vibrate at a frequency consistent with our thoughts and feelings. Gratitude has a frequency just like fear, anger, and worry have a corresponding frequency that's being sent out of us. This energy frequency is present 100-percent of the time.

Have you ever met a person for the first time and felt there was something that wasn't right about him or her? You couldn't put your finger on it, but something about that person just didn't align. In the same way, you meet people with whom you just click. They can light up the entire room by walking into it. They don't have to say or do anything. It's all about their vibrancy and the emotions.

You may not always find yourself in a favorable situation, but there is Biblical wisdom when Jesus said, "Agree with your adversary quickly" (Matthew 5:25, New King James Version). What does Jesus mean by this? It's all about eliminating your resistance, and replacing it with more positive emotions. When there is conflict in the midst of a negative situation, the tendency is to resist. However, 'to agree' means to synchronize yourself with something. Whatever you resist will persist, but once you accept something with an attitude of gratitude, you will be able to turn the feelings around for your own advantage.

The Space for Gratitude

Generally, gratitude only exists on an intellectual level rather than on emotional or spiritual level. People may be thankful (in their mind) for better jobs and more money, but that is not real gratitude. It is only one of the contents in the context of their experience.

When something is in the context of your life, it serves as the frame by which you understand how things occur to you. The context becomes the lens by which you see the world. You must set yourself up as a space of gratitude. Simply put, when you create yourself to be a space of gratitude means everything that you experience in your life is interpreted through gratitude.

Real gratitude is a state of being. It's not just an emotion that is dependent on what's going on outside of you. Gratitude must be the context that you are operating in so that you are thankful even when things don't go your way. It must be in every fiber of your blueprint.

Train yourself to exude gratitude in every thought, word, and action. Coming from that place of gratitude will help you reach your goals in life, and allow you to truly shift gears toward a more positive and better you. Be thankful and grateful of what works well in your life.

> **TRANSFORMATION PRINCIPLE 12:**
>
> **Be thankful and grateful of what works well in your life**

Embedding Gratitude into your Blueprint

Try this experiment for a week and see the change that happens in your emotions, perspective, and experiences. Start your morning with gratitude. Every day that you get out of bed, try to develop a consciousness aimed at it. What can you be thankful for in those moments? List at least five things you can be thankful for each day.

Truly, practicing a daily ritual of gratefulness will do wonders. This trains you to build gratitude into your blueprint. Recall the story of the prisoner in Brazil that I recounted earlier in the book. He was frightened at being in a foreign country and in prison. He prayed for freedom, and after a week, he was released. His gratitude, however, was short-lived. He began to get his life back together in Switzerland, and his thankfulness seemed to fade.

Like joy, you need to be grateful regardless of your external circumstances. This might be challenging at first, but it is part of the process of overwriting your blueprint. Start meeting people for no reason, just to see who they are and what they are doing. This eliminates so much of the stress associated with meeting people and making a good impression, and surprisingly, a lot of good usually comes out of such meetings. Just be yourself.

The Buddha once said, "All that we are is a result of what we have thought. The mind is everything. What we think, we become." Similarly, King Solomon of ancient times said, "For as he thinks in his heart, so is he" (Proverbs 23:7, New King James Version). Ralph Waldo Emerson also tells us, "A man is what he thinks all day long." Do you dwell in complaints and negativity, or do you dwell in thankfulness?

Make it a practice to have a genuine appreciation for everything around you, for all the triumphs, the losses, and the lessons learned. Dwelling on your mistakes and disappointments from the past will not serve you in the least but will only diminish your capacity to be grateful in the present.

When you're faced with unemployment, overdue bills, dysfunctional relationships, illness or any other devastating circumstance, declaring gratitude will become difficult. I can relate with this. How can you even begin when the pain around you is too much? You just do it. You just declare aloud the things you can be thankful for. Change the focus of your attention. In the beginning, these may seem like empty words. But the more you passionately search for things you can be grateful for, the more your perspective will widen to see what you're missing out on.

The Situation has Nothing to do with your Gratitude

Earl Nightingale said, "Learn to enjoy every minute of your life. Be happy now. Don't wait for something outside of yourself to make you happy in the future." You don't have to wait for something amazing to happen to be grateful. As he said, "learn" to experience the joy of gratitude right now, not tomorrow or when you finally have this or that. He tells us so that we can and should become masters of this skill. You don't need to wait until you're richer, healthier, thinner, or when you have more time for yourself, or when your last girlfriend or boyfriend comes back into your life. You need to be grateful for simply being who you are right now. Imagine yourself as a beggar again; what would you be thankful for?

No doubt, you'd be thankful if someone gave you a couple of cents in change, or treated you to a hot meal. But, since you're not a beggar, are you thankful for the couple of dollars you have in your purse, or the hot meal you'll be eating for dinner under your own roof?

Grumbling vs. Gratitude

When you act from a position of gratitude, you set in motion corresponding positive circumstances for your life. Moving from where you are to where you want to be begins with a change of attitude. A good place to start is by becoming grateful for the ability to think of the *possibility* of something new for your life. A lot of people are stuck with an attitude of grumbling; but if you find some good even when the bad is staring you in the face, your worldview will start to look up. Even when faced with an unpleasant situation, you can change the way you view it.

All situations are neutral when they occur; they gain a status as pleasant or unpleasant based on how you deal with it. Your treatment of a situation makes it to *become* that. If an unpleasant' situation occurs, you are not likely to face it with gratitude, because doing so would have transformed it. Transforming your way of thinking about it and receiving it will transform the situation.

If you come from a place of grumbling and discontent, then the negative thoughts that you exude will make you a co-creator of the events and situations happening around the world. Are you *being* a source of positive things or of negative things in the world? The LOA and the Law of Vibration operate in sync with each other. As you dwell in anger, bitterness, or frustration, you become a source of these emotions. If you want to change the conditions around you, you'll need to change your mind about them. When you operate in a context of gratitude, you will become a source of joy, love, and peace.

Gratitude and the LOA

Neville Goddard has something to say about gratitude and the Law of Attraction. He said that at times, one should picture the end goal and imagine himself attaining it. That end goal should be something that is a part of your master plan. Accept it in gratitude mentally, then watch it come to pass. Goddard believes that a person could invite and receive any condition in life from that position. But detachment may have to occur first between yourself and whatever is draining you of gratitude so that you can be open to inviting and receiving the good.

> **TRANFORMATION PRINCIPLE 10:**
>
> **Accept it in Gratitude Mentally, then Watch it Come to Pass.**

Is it an unemployment scare? Is it the fear of losing your spouse to an illness? Is it a looming bankruptcy? Detach yourself from these situations. The conditions don't define you or your joy. Let them go. It's only when you've set yourself apart from these things that you can clear your mind and summon an attitude of gratitude back into your space again. Moving away from the negative emotions toward the neutral ones is already a significant step toward being grateful.

Steps to Living in Gratitude Today

To incorporate the good into your own life and start giving thanks today, begin by being humble. Start focusing on what is working in your life right now; even if it's a small thing, like drinking a glass of water, taking a shower, shaving, or wearing freshly cleaned clothes. Pray for the people who helped make these things happen. Remember that everything and everyone is connected, so when you are grateful for something, you are capable of being grateful for everything.

Use your time wisely and multitask. You can begin to build on your life script while you do the dishes or drive to work. This will help you maintain your good life; at the same time, you begin ordering what you want in master plan clearer. The more time you devote to building your script, the stronger your thoughts and emotions will become, and the faster they will invite the manifestation of good into your reality.

In our Life Guide and Coaching programs, we emphasize the importance of building a life vision. We also tell our clients that building a life vision requires time, passion, and performance. In your case, you cannot build and achieve your master plan in ten minutes. It takes a significant amount of time, patience, and commitment to actually see it through. When you are idle, put your mind to work by building on the vision of your life script. Philip Lahm, the captain of the 2014 winning German soccer team at the World Cup in Brazil, told reporters that he had watched the video of the former German World Cup captain Lothar Matthäus holding the world cup back in 1990. He said he that he had watched the video over 100 times. He imagined with gratitude and joy what Matthäus must have felt in that moment. Lahm began to anticipate winning the World Cup before it was a reality. There was a lot of practice involved before his goal manifested, but real winners like him understand the power of feelings and well-being.

Emotion-Based Goal-Setting

When you write down your goal list, no doubt you will have a wide array of emotions attached to it. When you build out your life script, you must consider the related feelings that will come with the experiences, and infuse your list with them as well. While goals can energize and motivate you, you must also focus on the emotions your goals will bring you. Why do you want to achieve the goal, after all? You want the feeling that goes with it. It's not usually the luxury car that people want in and from it—they want the prestige that comes with it.

You can do this in your own life by imagining what it would feel like to finally have what your heart desires. Be grateful for the feelings, which will feed and overwrite your blueprint. The thing is that winners focus on their big dreams and then start to take daily step-by-step actions. Your life and goals for emotional freedom are no different. Dream. Practice. Build.

People often develop a grand vision, but don't follow through on the necessary steps toward attaining it because they didn't really want it enough to put work into it. They want immediate gratification. People tend to get discouraged when they do not see immediate change in their current situation after implementing a plan. However, holding on to the feelings of gratitude will enable you to endure the season of waiting, no matter how long.

MENTOR'S SECTION: MARIE FORLEO

Marie Forleo launched a one-woman business coaching practice in 2001 and then built a multi-million dollar empire. Her company focuses on helping small business and personal development training for women entrepreneurs. She also built a robust media platform, which extends the reach of her brand, from which she earned much recognition that she got invited to South Africa to mentor other young entrepreneurs there.

Forleo was able to create opportunity by building her brand ahead of her business. She taught me the importance of your personal brand. Because she had a clear brand, people know what to expect when she built her business.

In 2001, she quit her job in publishing to start a coaching business. In 2003, she kept coaching, but she also became an MTV hip-hop choreographer. While coaching, she became one of the world's first Nike Elite Dance Athletes. She was also able to author a self-published book *Make Every Man Want You* in 2006. She created the world's first digital training programs in 2007 and launched the first Rich Happy & Hot Mastermind, Virtual Coaching Program, and Live Event. In 2011, she flew to South Africa with Richard Branson to work with Virgin Unite. If there's somebody who exemplifies making her life count and pursuing her passions in life, it's Marie.

> **"Intuition rules. We trust our gut over everything else. We take big risks when it feels right and turn down revenue, opportunities and partnerships that, despite looking great on paper, give us that flash of intuitive doubt."**
>
> **- Marie Forleo**

Chapter 9
Live with Abundance

> *"Be yourself, but better yourself. Don't settle. Resist complacency. Continue to grow, learn, give, and develop. Never stop learning or giving."*
>
> - Craig Ballantyne

A Life of Abundance

A life of abundance all starts with a major decision. At this point, I would like to clarify that sacrifice, though not often discussed in books about LOA, is a major element. This period of examining your life is all about making a decision to live a life of abundance and freedom. I experienced a major epiphany when I decided to go into this "all in" without giving in to the fear of consequences. Closing all doors is very difficult and more than a little uncomfortable, but it will soon give way to sweet freedom.

I had never known the feeling I was experiencing at that point. I called it pure and true happiness. It is different from euphoria. It felt like being protected and fine all the time, nurtured and detached from the emotional rollercoaster that I had spent my life riding. It felt like the elusive rest I had been seeking in other things since I could remember.

I began to draw on a natural self-confidence to handle every challenge that arose in my life. I also learned to let go of the fear of uncertainty. In addition, the journey taught me to stay in the moment, because that would be the only way I could have any sense of what would happen in my future. Indeed, don't chase money let it come to you.

> **TRANSFORMATION PRINCIPLE 13:**
>
> **Don't Chase Money Let it Come to You.**

When you imagine a life of abundance, it's likely a life of enjoying constant inner peace and emotional freedom. If you reach this state, you will view your entire life—in all aspects—in a different light. Financially, you would see money as a means to an end, not an end in itself. Money and materialistic goods would not be your masters anymore. Money is important, but it should never drive your decisions; instead, it should work for you as the fuel that can power your self-built engine of purpose and life.

A Posture to Receive

Receiving is a completely different channel from ordering. With all the LOA books around, can you imagine all the orders out there from all the people who try to harness the power of the LOA? However, there is a receiving part of the game. To receive, you must prepare to experience resistance, because there will be plenty of it.

Take on a posture of openness with an unfettered imagination for what could be. Free yourself from generalized assumption of scarcity. Most of our lives we've operated in 'lack'. Do you remember the story of the millionaires in the dessert? When you're operating out of 'lack', you are desperate. You will give everything you have for a single bottle of water.

When you operate from a standpoint of 'lack', you are in survival mode. But when you're only operating to survive, your actions will be reactive rather than proactive. On the other hand, when you operate from a standpoint of abundance, you are peaceful and free to respond according to your master plan. Instead of operating in fear, you will operate with confidence.

When we view ourselves as fixed and limited, we feel that something will eventually run out. This attitude prompts us to seek and acquire more for ourselves no matter how much we already have. This also pushes us to constantly compete with other people. This way of being is led by the Ego. Scarcity-thinking and real scarcity lead to being in constant frenzy about the accumulation of resources. This way of thinking doesn't consider stepping on toes or violating other people's welfare along the way. But we live in a world that has enough to supply the needs of everyone.

Limitation is just the story of mainstream media. Just begin to focus on a world of abundance and love and you will start to experience it. Operate with a mindset of knowing that good is readily available; you will then be able to detach from it emotionally and take on a posture of receiving. That is one of the keys to a life of abundance. In order to have this said mindset, you just have to overwrite your blueprint and design it in such a way that you are capable of receiving what you desire.

Serendipity

There are no coincidences in life. When you set off on your own journey, you will begin to view the things, those you once thought to be coincidences, as serendipity. You will learn that everything is constantly moving to bring you to exactly where you're supposed to be. You will receive signs along the way to guide you to your next steps, but it takes intuition and courage to take those steps and move up the path.

These signs will appear in your consciousness after you've decided to step into your journey fully. Trusting your emotions prior to that is impossible, because your attachment to physical things will cause them to shift constantly according to the circumstances. Your inner attitude will always affect your outer actions. Therefore, you must establish inner peace and surrender to create an internal locus of control. Most people have an external locus of control in which everything is dependent on the external circumstance. Similarly, mastering your emotions is one important step in this process.

Breakdowns are not Problems

With a world around us that tries to minimize all risk, many of us have lost the ability and desire to step away from the comfort zone. Instead of moving forward and embracing uncertainty, we choose to be "safe". When things are difficult or don't go our way, we panic and react instead of respond.

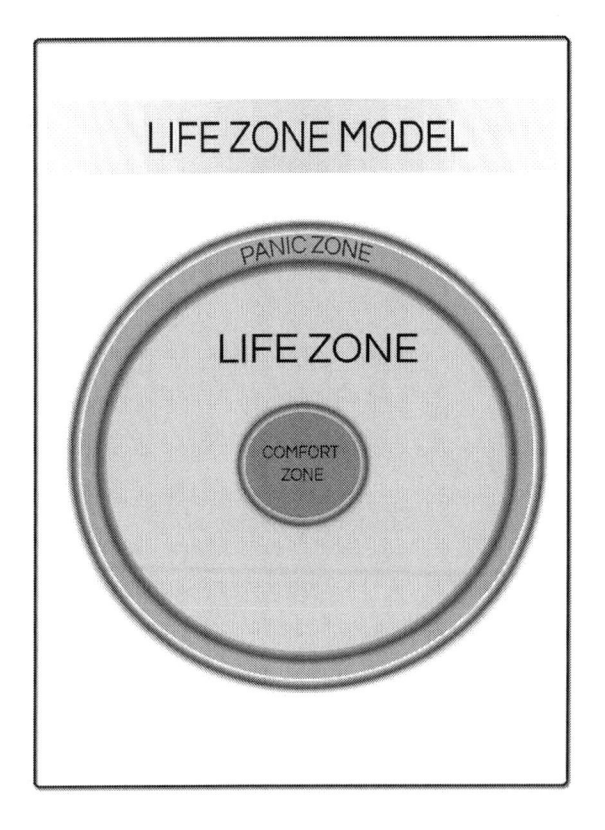

Figure 9 Life Zone Model

People who are in the rat race remain there because they are comfortable. When their lives are shaken, they move from the comfort zone to the panic zone. If a person is unaware of his emotions and unprepared to handle them, when disaster strikes internal chaos and panic will prevail. Only prepared people can stay calm. This is why preparation and training is a necessity. If the stock market crashes, people panic; those who are prepared can respond and make decisions based on emotional freedom.

How do you view life and circumstances when they do not go your way? Do you see them as problems or breakdowns? There's a difference. A problem tells you something is not right. The people around you may say to you that you have failed or that you are bound in a hopeless situation. But who defines what is 'right' and how things should be? 'Problems' are only what you make them in your mind. Consider instead viewing setbacks as breakdowns.

Breakdowns are temporary, hence fixable since something can and will be done to them. However, fixing them may require a little help from someone who knows how to approach the breakdown in the most effective way. The first step in approaching a breakdown is to *define it*. Once defined, they are already half-solved.

The second step is to *regenerate commitment* in your relationships. When you encounter a breakdown, it's easy to call it quits. You may, in fact, have already encountered seasons of lack, of disappointments, or of 'No', but it is in this part of the journey you will either recommit to your master plan and finish the race, or run. To lock your resolve into place and stand firm through the temporary setbacks, you should focus on your master plan. Then you will be inspired to move forward.

The third step is to *plan*. Prepare actions that will allow you to move closer to what you can do. Don't focus on what you don't have right now and don't fret about the things that aren't going your way.

The fourth step is to *act*. Once you've identified what you can do in the present, you must take a step toward it. As always, talk is cheap if not followed by action. Don't sulk in the corner or spontaneously break into tears about the woes of your life. Instead, focus on the possibilities, and then act to make them happen.

The Fear of Lack is the Denial of Vulnerability

Too often we see lack as a problem. We don't see it as breakdown that can be maximized and used for our purposes. We fear lack because we don't want to be in a place of uncertainties on money, for example, and where it will come from to pay the bills, or to pay for school. Lack opens the heart to vulnerability by the humble and often silent admission that we need help.

Sometimes, in our effort to avoid vulnerability, we "act" in a responsible manner, which many do by staying in jobs they dislike and by working for corporations and causes they don't believe in. This senseless busyness temporarily masks our vulnerability to admit that we are unhappy. It also keeps us running ragged in the rat race without thinking. We work hard but are unproductive; we are never forced to undergo a real change in our lives. We try to *look* good at the cost of sabotaging our most important goals in life.

Breakdowns are a Blessing

Now, before you put down the book and think, *this guy is crazy,* hear me out. Do you have the emotional freedom to view breakdowns as gifts? It's true—each breakdown is a gift. You can see these 'problems' as opportunities to do things differently. Each one is an open door to new possibilities. These breakdowns reveal the strength of your commitment to your master plan. When breakdowns happen under this new way of viewing them, you can assess yourself and improve in the areas in which you are weak or lacking.

> ***TRANSFORMATION PRINCIPLE 14:***
>
> ***You can see these 'problems' as opportunities to do things differently.***

Breakdowns open the door to action. When life is good and things are going well, there's no real need to commit. Nothing is forcing to you take a stand on what you believe; nothing is declaring who you actually want to be, because at the moment, life may feel absolutely fine. But the breakdowns force you to stop abruptly and reevaluate what you may have deluded yourself once again to think you had known and had been doing right as you sailed through life increasingly comfortably and perhaps apathetically—even after discovering that your past life had been an illusion of happiness.

When you come face to face with a 'problem', you are pushed to act upon your declared commitment. More importantly though, you are given the chance to view it as a 'breakdown' rather than something you cannot change. When you have no evidence that success is just around the corner, *that* is the time that faith must be reactivated. It is a time of testing your resolve to follow through on your desires.

When you have nothing and no one left to lean on, your commitment's nature and strength will be tested and revealed. If you see that it lacks, you mustn't tear yourself down. Pick yourself up, and resolve to do better, and express gratitude that you were given this breakdown opportunity to mirror your true motives and desires with clarity for your own good.

When attention is focused on the wrong things, such as 'problems', hopelessness will soon follow. You will increasingly feel that the situation is beyond your power. Attachment to wealth, or an intense longing and desire for it, will cause you to either work endlessly in search of it or become despondent as a victim. If you choose the latter, you will accept that things just happen.

When you operate as a slave, you set into motion a cruel cycle of emotional turmoil and despair. The only way to address this is to allow yourself to be vulnerable. You do this by admitting your unhappiness and seeing the illusions you've believed in your life.

Gaining Leverage

You don't have to push for things when they don't happen immediately or the way you expected them to. That situation is not a sign of failure or a limitation; it's also not an impossibility. You can still move forward on—or toward— the path that you've set out on.

Richard Branson, founder of Virgin Records, used to travel extensively. He saw a lot to be desired in the service and experience of his airline travels. But instead of becoming disgruntled and angry about his bad experiences, he gratefully accepted the "breakdown". In so doing, he found a new opportunity. He picked himself up and established his own airline—Virgin Atlantic.

Successful people see every breakdown as an opportunity to innovate or to create something better. These people are not born with a special gene that allows them to be successful or to see things more optimistically. They become that way because they have seen the illusion of life, and they learned that they must be responsible for their lives. They also resolved to transform their minds to live by new emotions and ways of thinking. When they evaluate their lives, they approach themselves with a constant question of how they can gain rise above their current circumstances and situations. When you look at your own life, what can you do to make the best out of your circumstances? This is especially true for the breakdowns. You must ask yourself, "What can I do to gain leverage from this breakdown"?

When Branson returned from the maiden transatlantic flight of his new airplane, he discovered that his credit line had been cancelled. But he didn't take it as a divine sign that he should never have started out on this journey or that he should abandon his business pursuits. Instead, he quickly sought out and found other means to fund his business endeavor, eventually acquiring a new credit line many times higher than his previous one.

You see it's all a matter of perspective. Branson's experiences serve to remind us that we can see a problem as something that happens to you. It also reminds us that we are powerless to change. At some point, it also tells us to see a problem as an opening act that initiates the greatness in you to rise up and prove itself. You can see these breakdowns as new possibilities for abundance.

The Essence of Love

Online dating and matchmaking platforms are becoming popular as people become increasingly starved for love as though it were a race. But what is true love? Does love necessarily involve a romantic partner? Your prince or princess charming may be out there, but he or she might be somebody who thinks he or she *needs* somebody for attention and love and self-worth, maybe just like you. My manifesto is: Love yourself first so that you can start to experience a completely different relationship. It must be an emotionally free relationship with you, without the drama of life in the rat race.

I'm forever indebted to a special woman I'll call Angel Queen, who asked me, "Do you think we are a good match *in essence*?" She didn't ask if we matched in terms of intellect or interest and hobbies, physical appearance, or financial capacity. Instead, she asked if we matched at our cores. I will never forget this question because it changed my life. The next morning, I started a new company venture with the brand name Essential Rich.

Your essence is your core purpose in life and your well-being. It should dictate your actions. Do not follow the example of some people who are not courageous enough to let their essence shine for the world to see. Our essence is the deepest part of ourselves, and because it is deep within, we always endeavor to keep it hidden because. We think that our essence reveals our capabilities, behaviors, and identity—things that we think do not align with what others expect of us. With a desire to maintain the status quo, we hide who we are and we hide our essence.

The Power of Connection

Our life is designed in such a way that it is connected with a higher being. We are rational beings gifted with emotions; we are God's creations expected to care for the rest of His creations. As the story of Creation in the Bible goes, God said, "Let us make man in *Our image*, according to *Our likeness*; let them have dominion over the fish of the sea, over the birds of the air, and over the cattle, over all the earth and over every creeping that that creeps on the earth" (Genesis 1:26, New King James).

In essence, we were created in the image and likeness of God, which makes us divine. But because the system of the Ego and flesh has consumed us, our desire for the material and for status has caused us to lose sight of our true essence. When we reconnect with the higher power deep within, we can experience the wholeness of our beings.

The system holds humanity back. It tells us that we're incomplete, therefore are in need of many things to *feel* and to *be* complete. Advertisements convince us that we need cars, beauty, and any other luxuries to experience a sense of wholeness. These needs, we are told, will be met by acquiring physical wealth. In this way, we blindly chase after it in hopes of finding fulfillment. We acquire so many things yet remain incomplete as ever.

LIVE WITH ABUNDANCE

The thing you crave, without knowing it, has been within you all your life. You are already a complete being. Abundance resides within, and you and I are essentially rich. Unfortunately, many simply do not recognize the integrity of their essence; therefore, they never come to realize that abundance lies within their reach if they only look inward. Discovering and reconnecting with the divine can move you towards becoming a co-creator of your life with the God who created you.

Speak out Loud

As you reach your goal of emotional freedom, you will want to share this message with the world. To share the secret that you have discovered is one of your greatest desires. It is also one of your greatest responsibilities, which is freeing the world from the rat race.

The ball will be in your court. By now, you must concur that success is not found in the pursuit or the acquisition of material wealth; instead, it is found in the significance of the mark you leave on the world. That is the measure of true success—a life lived true to self and thus loving others in the truest way while sharing your freedom.

Knowing you essence will result in recognizing and developing your master plan. Developing your master plan is greatly connected with knowing your interests and talents. You no longer have to be insecure about what you want to do in your life. An abundant life naturally results from pursuing and living your purpose in life.

Your essence is your true wealth. Through your inner strength, creativity, vulnerability, passions and talents your true wealth will come to manifest itself. All throughout my coaching experience, I have observed that all people are talented or gifted in some area, but they are often too afraid to pursue their gifts and purposes because they fear finding out what they lack.

Because they rely heavily on the current financial system, they are left stuck in jobs they don't love and in enslaving situations. They would rather trust the monetary system than put their faith in the existence of the LOA. This attachment to material things creates the fear of 'lack' and keeps them in the race. When it is 'lack' that you fear, it is 'lack' that will be delivered.

Courage to Stand Up

Take a step of faith. Pursue your passion. Chase the dream that you have buried for so long or perhaps you have never realized. Discover and develop that which you are actually good at doing. Start that business that you've only ever 'thought' of.

Perhaps you'd like to start a website that shares your joys, passions, and ability with others. You need to step out of the comfort zone and get in front of others. Don't be content with your 9-to-5 job, because you are not necessarily happy in it.

Don't be afraid to ruffle feathers or to go against the system. You must not fear venturing into something you love. Instead of working to acquire money, you must work toward pursuing your purpose.

Grab hold of courage and show the world and the doubters what you can do. Don't do it for the money—wealth will follow when you're passionate and committed to a cause. Do it instead as a contribution to the world and to yourself. Step out to discover yourself and see the joy in serving others.

Now, you may be reading this and thinking, *I'm not cut out to be an entrepreneur* or *I'm not cut out to sell my own products or services—I'm just not like that.* Don't think of it like that, because you are not selling a product or a service, you're offering your inner talents to the world. You're sharing your source of joy with others, whether or not in your own business or working for someone else; just make sure you are doing what you love.

Life is a Contact Sport

We are all interconnected with each other. Therefore, you must learn how to offer your value to others. Remember that to have a successful business, you must not focus simply on making a sale of a product; instead, focus on how you can serve humanity. In the end, a sale is necessary because without a sale you can never survive in that job. But keep the customer instead of the money as the focus and the sales will come.

Staying in a job because you feel there's no alternative is wrong. Not only are you not being true to yourself; you're also denying the world the opportunity to benefit from your unique talents and skills. To find fulfillment through living a life of integrity, you must leave that job and do something that feeds your heart. Do that and you're a step closer to living in emotional stability and freedom.

We must learn to connect with people 'just because'. The old way of thinking dictated meeting and connecting with people who could *do* something for you. Change that mindset and meet people for who they are—interesting, funny, and unique. Don't approach them with expectations of what you can gain by your interaction with them. Become interested in their dreams even if they find your asking strange.

Transform your mind, so you may in turn transform theirs by your new approach of 'exchanging money for time.' Once you've decided to live in abundance, a box or a fixed set of definitions should never limit you, even if people find you odd. Muster up the courage to stand out and be distinguished.

Get your Audience

My journey led me here, and this book has found its way into your hands for a reason. It's your turn now to go on your own journey and to find your own audience. First, you need to be authentic and show integrity in what you do and in what you stand for. When you operate with integrity, you will be able to find people who can bring you closer to accomplishing your master plan.

I've been on this journey for the sake of learning and joy. Living the old life, I observed that my energy was constantly being zapped because nothing was ever enough to revive it. But now that I am pursuing my passion and doing what I love, there is a new energy and vibrancy for life created. I call this "Free Energy Power." This power is the one that has fueled me, and will also fuel you, in going further and further in the journey.

To think that some people are just lucky enough to find a job doing something they love is a misconception. If you think or believe that statement, you will be the person settling for what you have. But you deserve to live a life doing something you love for a living.

At *Essential Rich*, we hope to share this Free Energy Power as a lifestyle brand. Essential Rich stands for unconditional love and abundance. Operating from this vantage will allow you to leverage any situation that comes your way. In so doing, you can live out your life with purpose. Essential Rich is about living in freedom with the possibility of being able to do anything you desire to do.

Essential Rich aims to help others discover and express their own purposes in life. When you learn to express yourself freely and reveal who you are, you will gain new power and energy. When you free yourself from the fear of 'lack' and detach yourself from physical wealth, you will be able to pursue activities that are simply you. Consequently, you will forever be free to be yourself.

Believing in Abundance Leads to Emotional Freedom

Have you heard of Pareto's Law? According to that law, only 20 percent of your output (which includes your energy, your time, and your other resources) produces 80-percent of the input in your life. For example, in a single day, only 20-percent of what you do can actually takes you 80-percent closer to reaching your dreams.

When it comes to business, only 20-percent of your leads are actually generating 80-percent of your sales. Only 20-percent of your investments are generating 80-percent of your ROIs (return of investment). This, therefore, tells us to streamline our systems of doing things, and work smarter rather than harder.

People who aren't busy often feel insignificant, and so they try to fill their days with 'doing' even when it's not particularly productive. Because they lack emotional freedom, they feel guilty when they're not working hard for money. The thought of working only a few hours a day and trusting that by doing what they love the money would come would be completely unbelievable to them. However, this is the reality of many people who have attained emotional freedom.

They are no longer bound by the old system of work and finances; in fact, they have pursued their own unique calling. As a result, they experience happiness, joy, and inner peace; they also have time to think because they are no longer driven to work all day long. Emotional freedom will empower you to put this principle to work. You will be confident and secure in accomplishing the things that matter, knowing that you're focusing on something that will ultimately pay later.

If you think about your typical workday, you may spend eight to ten hours in the office five days per week for years. However, how much of the workday were you able to spend doing something productive? Looking back at those years, many people wish they had had more time to spend with family and friends, or on hobbies that they could have enjoyed. You might say, "Well, I'd love to do that, but I have to work." Solution: Create the situation that allows you to live and love the work you do. Remember, when you're operating in abundance, money won't be an issue anymore.

Symptoms of a New Blueprint

Once you decide to leave on the transformational journey, make sure you commit fully and close all other doors behind you need to focus on your path ahead. Abundance cannot co-exist with lack. You must choose. If you want to move forward in your emotional journey, start with closing all doors in areas where you have feared 'lack'. Initially, you will likely wonder if you have broken free, or if you will fall back into the past—but that's okay. However, once you've sealed yourself in emotional freedom, you can never and will never fall back. Showdowns may happen, but you will overcome them.

Sealing in your mindset of abundance allows you to move forward in integrity. The following are the signs, which will show you that you have already sealed your new blueprint for abundance:

- You are no longer attached to outcomes and are willing to be surprised

- You are committed to living in love, rather than in fear

- You can be honest about your personal feelings
- You can accept the responsibility for having created your past emotions
- You are willing to let go of hurt, blame, and anger
- You are curious rather than judgmental
- You are present in the present

Sealing a New Blueprint

What can you do to seal your blueprint with emotional freedom, inner peace, and abundance? Sealing your blueprint requires your full attention and consciousness so you won't hurt yourself early on. Be kind to yourself, and let a new strong foundation begin to grow and take shape. Yes, your Ego will put up a fight, but the strength you need is already within you.

Albert Einstein said that insanity was "doing the same thing over and over again and expecting different results." When you step out of your comfort zone, you can then step into your courage zone. You may be stepping into an unknown way of life, but this time, you can author your life. You won't have to settle for what circumstances and conditions dictate for you.

Your life will be a true expression of who you are. Pray and ask for protection. Pray in gratitude. Pray for mentors to guide you. Then let it happen.

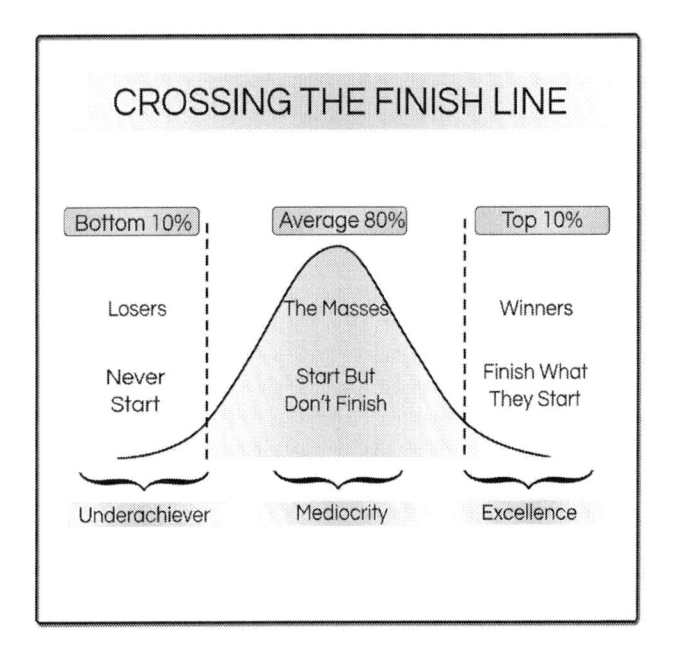

Figure 10: Crossing the Finish Line

Adapted from Phil Laut and Andy Fuehl's book, *Wealth Without a Job*, this figure reveals that you can only cross the finish line when you finish what you started and operate in excellence. Most people, however, are stuck in mediocrity. They start something great, but never have the commitment or the patience to finish it. Then there are those who are scared to even begin. You want to be a winner and it's possible through emotional freedom.

MENTOR'S SECTION: STEVEN SPIELBERG

As a child, Steven Spielberg was an amateur filmmaker. Today, he is one of the most well-known directors of our time. This guy started shooting anything in front of him as an eight-year-old boy using his dad's 8-millimeter camera. But there was more to his story than having a passion for filmmaking at such a young age.

He was the oldest of four kids. Spielberg's parents used to fight all the time. His father was also an engineer who was not home usually. He longed to connect with his father, but his longing was prevented because Spielberg usually had poor grades at school. He did not have a happy family life, which was a major struggle in his life.

As a form of escape from the relational dysfunction in his family, Spielberg escaped by creating a fantasy world through his movies. He spent much of his time making films. Spielberg did not pay much attention to his studies. Being the only Jew in the neighborhood, other kids also bullied him. His childhood was not easy on him.

When Spielberg was in college, he took a summer job as a clerical intern at the Universal Studios. After dropping out of college, he continued to hang out on the lot. However, since the guards knew he was not an intern anymore, he would encounter trouble with them. It was no surprise that he was innovative even at that age. Spielberg would dress in a suit and tie and walk right up to the gate like he belonged there.

Once on the lot, Spielberg would introduce himself to actors, producers, and directors. He watched how movies were shot and soaked up everything he could. Spielberg said he probably got kicked off a set every day. However, rejection did not stop him from learning. He kept on going to pursue his master plan. He knew he wanted to make films. He pursued a passion, not the salary.

Spielberg viewed obstacles as showdowns to his success. He overcame his Ego and won these showdowns. His films include *Jaws, Close Encounters of the Third Kind, Indiana Jones, ET, Poltergeist, The Color Purple, Schindler's List, Jurassic Park,* and *Saving Private Ryan.*

I dream for a living.

- Steven Spielberg

Chapter 10
Let it Happen

People look to an event like to Olympics and think that the gold medal is the ultimate goal but the process to get there is far more important.

– Anonymous

The Gourage to Let Go

This entire journey has been a tug-of-war within me. The Ego consistently fought against every decision and action I made back then. But power comes from gaining the courage to let go.

This part of the journey is about losing intellectual control. I realized that I can't let things, places, or people dictate my happiness. True happiness and success always depended on my willingness to let go of things I couldn't control. I needed to focus my energy, instead, on things that I had the power to influence, such as my finances, my relationships, my circumstances, and my environment.

We have grown up in a society in which one is considered a winner if he has all the power and the control. This is the illusion most people operate by in life and business. The *need* to be in control and to plan every action dominates the day, leading to distraction and forgetfulness of living in the here and now.

We strive for control of every detail in our lives in a way that our goals become our motivation for living. We also become stubborn to achieve them. This situation is both beneficial and detrimental since it initiates the forming of strong commitments toward a vision in life. Apart from that, it can also fixate you on achieving things in exactly the way you've imagined, leaving no room for life to happen. When this happens, disappointments will often follow.

But even so, you need to be specific about what you want for your life's master plan. Your life script will provide you with a definite destination. Take note that an individual with a higher level of consciousness understands that thoughts and beliefs create their lives. You have the power to stay focused on your purpose.

But you must also be faithful and flexible to allow life to work and to let the LOA do what it does best. In addition, you should be open to all the good that will show up in life, even those things that you didn't necessarily expect. On a final note, develop the courage to let go of the 'hows' and the 'whys', so you can have the power to just 'be'.

The Bank of Life

Everyone has a 'Bank of Life.' Like every other bank, it accepts deposits into accounts.' However, for it to be successful, the 'account holder' must be aware of what he or she is depositing into this account. What good is it to deposit a piece of cheese into an account that is designed to hold money?

The cheese will begin to stink and soon fill the whole bank with the rotting stench. This is exactly what happens when people accumulate unhealthy emotions, such as fear, insecurity, and negativity, which are not meant to be deposited. Instead, they fill us with an insufferable stench that so much of society has gotten used to and has come to expect. How will changing what you deposit into your personal account change your life? What do you need to fill your account in the Bank of Life?

Your account should be filled with faith and love. Faith in yourself, faith in what you're doing, and faith in the people you love is imperative for right living. But above all else, you must have faith in the power that exists; you must also know that life will always be what you make it. A person who lacks faith is insecure and will be easily shaken by circumstances. Lacking faith increases the chains of bondage and keeps you from experiencing true emotional freedom.

Like any account, you need to manage this 'Bank of Life' wisely and make sure that credit is not accumulating against you. Eliminate fears, both large and small. At our deepest cores, faith is the most natural response; fear, however, is completely unnatural in our originally created states. We were created to have faith.

Fear is a denial of our essence and goes against everything good within us. Fear claims that the Universal Law doesn't exist. Faith, on the other hand, allows you to allow life to come to you, even in times and ways that you don't understand. Faith is knowing that everything that comes as a result of your emotional freedom is good for you.

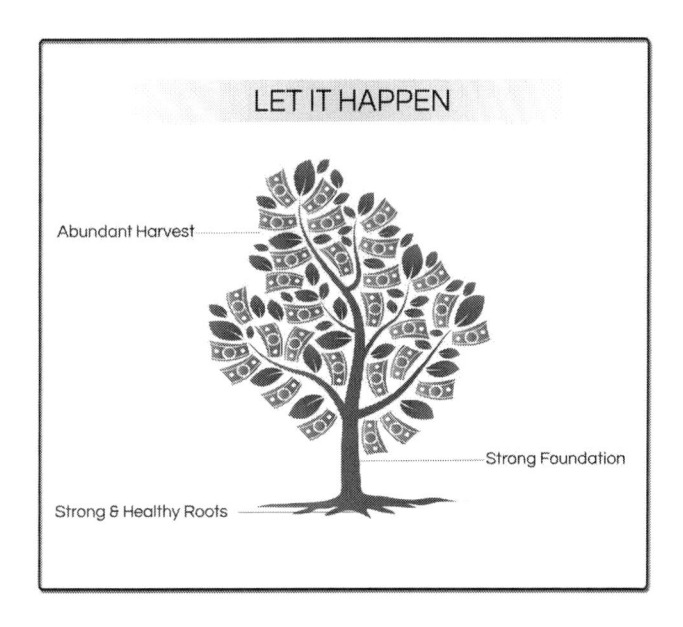

Figure 11: Money Tree

This is the Money Tree that also represents the Creade™ logo. You will reap the harvest of whatever you sow. If you sow abundance, you will reap abundance. But you must nurture the tree so that it can grow strong, healthy roots, and wait patiently as the tree develops strong foundations. The harvest will always come in the proper season.

The Law of Allowing

According to the Law of Allowing, you can powerfully and passionately focus on how the LOA can turn your vision into reality. You and I have been born into a world of choice. The beauty of life is that it always gives you the opportunity to discover your passion and purpose. You were born so that you can work on yourself.

Though the world will tell you otherwise, you are perfectly made. Therefore, you can be happy with what and who you are. You can create your own happiness and fulfillment through the LOA, but for utmost effectiveness, you need to acknowledge and recognize your power to create. If there are things in your life that you wish were different, then you can create that reality for yourself because life is an endless process. The only way you can truly perform in your life is to allow yourself to participate with the LOA in the process of creating your realities.

The Tent and the Rain

Among the five elements, water is the strongest since it represents feelings (fire is to power, air intellect, and earth materialism). How often do your own feelings overpower your life decisions?

Feelings have the main say in the use of your power, intellect, and wealth. Imagine going on a camping trip. Suddenly, you are stuck in a downpour. If you've dug a ditch around your tent, you will be able to direct your water in such a way that you can actually maximize the rainfall and utilize it as a blessing. If you have brought any containers with you, then you can store the water and use it. Abundance will always come to you.

The rain is a symbol of the harvest. If you're prepared for it and wait for it patiently, you don't need to buy water and take it with you on the trip. You just need to focus on containing the rainfall and letting it flow naturally so you can use it.

You can use this abundance concept in real life. You should always be prepared for the rain; when you're prepared, you won't react. Instead, you will simply allow it to happen and make the best use of it; after all, you will already have the different tools in place to gather the blessings. The bottom line is this: you need to prepare to let life happen. You don't have to chase money. You just have to let it flow to you.

Let it Come in Its Own Way

After placing your 'order', it's time to surrender your control for how it will come. Don't stress on the things that are missing in your life right now; in addition, don't focus on the impossibilities of this season. Instead, focus on what you can do right now. Direct your attention to what is possible in your current season. Stay calm and relaxed and let the world around you provide you with what you need to work on today. A German saying reads, "Der Mensch denkt, Gott lenkt", which means "Humans think, God guides".

You don't need to figure out time frames. Everything happens at the right time and in the right season. If you've asked for a specific thing and it didn't come at the time you expected, just know that something better would come, something that will serve everyone involved. Always start with the intention that people will always be blessed by the blessings in your life. Take the focus off of yourself and live.

> **TRANSFORMATION PRINCIPLE 15:**
>
> ***Take the focus off of yourself and live.***

What you Resist will Persist

The more you resist something, the more it will persist in your life. Resistance is a powerful thing that sucks all the energy and life right out of you. Yet people often dwell upon resistance. For example, if you fear that you won't get married in the future, you are resisting growing old alone. As you resist this fear of the future, you operate *in* fear trying to prevent this future from coming to pass. Your subconscious mind does not honor negations.

Even as you think, *I don't want to be single forever*, it picks up 'single' and 'forever'. Likewise, when you resist bankruptcy because of your attachment to physical wealth, you think, *I don't want to be broke.* Your subconscious mind will only pick up, 'broke.'

Imagine a sink full of dirty dishes. You walk past it, hesitant to look at it and not wanting to admit it's there. You resist it because you don't want to deal with it. The next morning, the dirty dishes are still there; contrary to your hopeful wishes, the dishes did not magically clean themselves. They persisted in lying in your sink waiting to be cleaned. Indeed, what you resist still persists.

So stop resisting and let your life happen. Face your fears and deal with your struggles. It's only when you surrender every resistance in your body that you'll be able to perform in life. Be still and relax. Instead of focusing on your anxieties and worries in life, direct your attention to something you enjoy. Meditate on your life script. Envision your master plan and picture yourself living the life that you've always imagined.

I like to go hiking and enjoy wellness spas. I like to intentionally do relaxing activities because they clear my mind of all the negativity. They empower me to let go of any resistance that the Ego creates within me. In this relaxed state of mind, I step closer to realizing my vision. I use this time to build on my life script.

The details are building the bigger picture, even if you can't see it at the moment. When you're facing a negative situation, look inside for peace and for something that will calm you down. Remind yourself of the beautiful vision that's ahead of you. Whatever showdowns you're experiencing right now, remember that they're just a part of the bigger picture.

Your Life Mailbox

The LOA allows you to 'order' what you want to experience in your life, and the Law of Allowing prepares you to 'receive' the delivery. The Law of Allowing is a natural part of the LOA. So pay attention to what you're broadcasting out during the season while waiting for your delivery.

If you're operating in a desperate mode of ordering, you'll forget about receiving. You might have received 'abundance' in your mailbox but forgot to take it into your house because you're on the phone complaining that your 'order' hasn't arrived yet. Once you've made the order you can expect it to arrive, though the method by which it arrives may be unexpected. Don't send back the package without unpacking it.

Most of us get the 'ordering' part, but we tend to misunderstand what kind of attitude we have for 'receiving' the delivery. People are constantly in the 'ordering' mode. They demand instant gratification.

Therefore, I advise that you work on yourself. When you're prepared to receive the gift, you'll recognize it easier when it finally arrives rather than being caught off-guard. When you wait with this kind of expectancy, the possibilities for the blessings that will arrive are endless.

Roadblocks to Delivery

The attitudes we hold in receiving the delivery of our master plans serve as blockades during the period of waiting. Turn on the curiosity about the life-taking place around you and refuse to stagnate.

Be a student of life and invest in learning. Be curious, always ready to remove the wrapping paper of whatever comes to you joyously. A lot of times we receive something that might come in the form of a problem or a disappointment, so we send it away because we ordered breakthroughs, not problems. But sometimes the best blessings come wrapped in packages of bumps and bruises, or pain and tears, so that you can learn something and grow through the process. Oftentimes the 'problems' prepare us to receive the breakthroughs.

Don't lose yourself in the wrapping paper and give up by throwing the entire package away. The LOA always works. People who lack gratitude and patience seldom find the gift hidden in the packaging of challenges and tests. Learn to become aware of the season you're in.

During the season of waiting, be patient and expectant. As you wait for the delivery, prepare yourself. It takes discipline to endure the waiting process. Nevertheless, it is this endurance that will see you through to the harvest you've been waiting for.

> **TRANSFORMATION PRINCIPLE 16:**
>
> **As you wait for the delivery, prepare yourself.**

Play Big

By playing big, you are able to reject the need to understand everything. Playing big requires that you don't settle but perform. Avoid the small mindset that rejects risks. Sometimes time makes people give up because they are afraid that they'll be disappointed. However, faith allows you to know for certain that you will receive, regardless of your current circumstance.

The Bible says that "Faith is the substance of things hoped for, the evidence of things not seen" (Hebrews 11:1, New King James). Your current circumstances may prevent you from seeing that your breakthrough could be coming at any moment. Nevertheless, faith allows you to keep on going through the rain and fog.

MENTOR'S SECTION: JORDAN BELFORT

Jordan Belfort, stockbroker and sales trainer, had a natural talent for sales at an early age. In 1987, he started selling stocks; by 1989 he was already running his own investment operation Stratton Oakmont. The company made millions illegally because it defrauded the investors. The Securities Exchange Commission began efforts to stop the company's errant ways in 1992. In 1999, Belfort pleaded guilty to securities fraud and money laundering. He was also sentenced in 2003 to four years in prison, but he only served 22 months. He published his first memoir, *The Wolf of Wall Street* in 2008.

He recounts in his book the point in his life when he was attached to wealth. During this time, he spent lavishly by buying mansions, sports cars, and other expensive things. He also developed a serious drug problem and as a result got into several accidents.

Belfort's company had the motto, "Don't hang up until the customer buys or dies." Because their philosophy is based on hard sell and money-driven tactics, the success and immediate gratification was short-lived.

After prison, Belfort wrote his memoir and talked about his meteoric rise and crash in the financial world. After having experienced the consequences of get-rich-quick schemes, he directed his energies to pursuing something more than making money. He pursued living a life that expresses and maximizes where he's naturally great. He changed his ways and now operates his own company that provides sales training and markets Straight Line training programs that are aimed at building wealth.

> **"I believe in total immersion, if you want to be rich, you have to program your mind to be rich. You have to unlearn all the thoughts that were making you poor and replace them with new thoughts – rich thoughts."**
>
> **– Jordan Belfort**

Chapter 11
Meet your Future Self

Your net worth is your network.

Unknown

Why Professional Athletes have Coaches

It's always the professionals who have coaches, not the amateurs. Think about an athlete. Those who keep their sport as a hobby don't seek help. They just play their games for fun.

But the one who wants to succeed at his sport always hires a coach, because he knows that he can only get better with the help of someone who has been there, and who knows how to get to the top. Life, sports, business, health, money, spirituality, entrepreneurship, writing, and marketing are popular fields that require coaches. They serve to help people become better at what they do or at what they want to do.

Successful people recognize that they need help. They have a winning attitude and won't settle to just get ranked. They have a burning desire to win. How do they get there? Coaches.

A winning attitude requires inner growth in a person's character, emotions, and personality. Sometimes athletes experience defeat; if they see the defeat as a permanent state, they'll stop training and give up. But successful athletes also know that it's through defeat that they learn as they go back and review why they lost. The defeat might have been because of poor form or that the timing was off.

Pointing out Blind Spots

Who do you think between Tiger Woods and his coach is a better golfer? Tiger Woods is definitely the better golfer. He would probably beat his coach every day of the week. However, he still invests in a coach because he knows that no matter how great he is at his sport, he'll always have blind spots.

His coach is there to help him analyze why he may have lost in an all-important game. There will always be areas about his performance that he cannot see or refuses to see. Therefore, he needs an unbiased, professional third party to point out.

In an organization, many companies recognize the value of mentoring. Usually mentoring is a critical part of success planning. Managers scout for leadership potential in their subordinates and pick out someone they can train to become the next leader in the company. Managers are able to point out what their employees lack and what they need to develop to succeed in leadership positions.

Therefore, they work with their employees to bridge this performance gap. In contrast, coaches are not consultants. They are only guides; some of them are role models in their own lives. However, most coaches do not make enough to pay the bills. That is why I offer my coaching clients a unique education, which includes marketing and important real-life business matters.

Have you ever experienced defeat? Who was there for you to help you pick up the pieces? Honestly, it's good to have people there who can speak encouragement and wisdom back into your life. When you might get stuck in negative or destructive habits, you must endeavor to break free.

Imagine a person who's having a heart attack. He cannot do CPR on himself, but needs other people to help him. In the same way, those who are slowly or rapidly facing an unknown future need help to break free from negative habits and limiting beliefs. Mentors help people perform better in life and business.

A Growing Field

Choosing a coach should be approached with reverence. It is not a hastily made decision, but one that is carefully thought out. First, know where you want to go. Next, find someone who inspires you through his or her own life and journey. Your mentor and coach are like your future self.

People generally choose a coach whom they want to emulate, not as a direct copy but as someone whom they can aspire to be like, while maintaining their own essence. If you want to lose weight, will you find someone who consistently overeats and has weight problems? No, you'll go to someone who's physically fit and has taken the steps to get him back in shape.

Understanding the difference between a coach and a consultant is really important. A real coach has mastered specific areas of his own life. If you want to be coached in investments, the best coach would be someone who was deeply in debt and found his way out. If you want to be a great spouse and parent, someone who has left a wild lifestyle behind and committed to marital fidelity would probably benefit you.

I refer to life coaches and mentors as Life Guides, because that is what they do. They guide their mentee in much the same way that a Sherpa leads a mountaineer safely to the summit of his choice. A life guide will support you and take your performance to the next level. Therefore, you should always go to someone who depicts the essence of what or who you want to *become*.

Your chosen coach should not be *shy to talk about his own transformation*. To ensure that they can take you where you want to go, make sure that any potential life guide is living an authentic life; the one you choose should be honest and open about his or her life path. As you get to know a person, you will discover either of these scenarios: they are only revealing the good and safe parts of their lives while hiding the skeletons in the closet and they might be truly authentic about who they had been and how they got to where they are now.

Ultimately, you decide where to go. A life guide won't carry you around or take you where you don't want to go. It's a relationship of walking side by side. Life guides don't do the work; they simply equip you with the right mindset and wisdom so you may perform well.

> **TRANSFORMATION PRINCIPLE 17:**
>
> **Life guides don't do the work; they simply equip you with the right mindset and wisdom so you may perform well.**

Your own experience will be your best teacher; but the experience of others will help you navigate your life down the most effective and sure course toward the end you seek. My mission is to help and guide people to transform their lives and liberate themselves from negative thoughts. If only people could begin to understand that unconditional love and connection to a higher self results in better business performance, they would find themselves in sync with a higher will. I want to spread a message of transformation and unconditional love pertaining to personal and business life.

The Life Entrepreneur Academy

Life itself is an entrepreneurial endeavor. An entrepreneur is someone who sets up a business and who invests to make a profit and to enjoy a better quality of life financially. He then reinvests part of his profit again into new ventures. He does so in hopes of achieving a harvest in return. Similarly, you invest your time, your energy, and your resources. Regardless if you're a business owner, an employee, or unemployed, you are an entrepreneur of life. The question is what kind of life-entrepreneur are you?

Out of my passion for life and a desire to share the new wealth I had found in achieving emotional freedom, I started the Life-Entrepreneur Academy to guide people to being better life performers and to following their own purposes in life. A key part of the content we teach combines self-development with regular and down-to-earth business practices like marketing, sales conversions, and more. Our programs are dedicated to helping people reach a higher level of consciousness and allow them to move forward in their lives so they can, in turn, help others move forward in their lives by becoming life guides themselves.

The programs are set-up for results. For those candidates who are ready to let go of old habits and start their own journeys in the order of the one I outlined in this book, we provide a guarantee of success. Our boot camp-like programs do not support illusions of change while one remains in the comfort zone. We do not lead you into anything harmful, but self-discipline, humbleness, performance, and decisive dedication are imperative. Our program is here to equip you to prepare, endure, and perform at elite levels.

Essential Matching in Relationships and Life

Different people have different master plans and blueprints by which they operate. So how do you find the best life coach for yourself? I would advise that you find someone whose master plan and blueprint resemble yours. This is called "Essential Matching."

The search for a life guide is a search for compatibility, like finding a spouse. Your essence is your nature. Your essence speaks about your nature. Your essence is your *being*. Who do you want to *become* in the future? To answer this, choose one who has already *become* whom you want to be so that he or she can guide you on your journey there.

> **TRANSFORMATION PRINCIPLE 18:**
>
> ***Choose a person who has already become who you want to be so that he or she can guide you on your journey there.***

Certainly, you will want to connect with those who are your essential matches. In a relationship, the basis of your connection is not on being physically, intellectually, or financially compatible. Instead, you should be essentially compatible with your partner. However, your mentor should be a step ahead of you in terms of the journey you will walk. No two people can be on exactly the same path, but paths can be similar. If you will go ahead of someone in your emotional journey, that person will likely not be the best person to follow as your life guide.

Mentors Took me Through the Journey

It's easy to get lost. I experienced that myself. But the life guides I had in my life helped me to stay focused on where I should go. Life guides can speak positivity and encouragement into your life, eventually refreshing you to continue on your life path. I allowed myself to be mentored by people who had achieved something great in their own lives. I did so because I wanted to accomplish something great on my own. I wanted to emulate emotionally and financially wealthy people for what they manifest within the world to which they have given their contributions.

In the process, I realized that I needed to study the lives of successful people and learn what they did differently from other people. By studying their lives, I allowed them to mentor me through their life experiences.

A real mentor is not afraid to tell you honestly about the truth. He will risk offending you for the sake of correcting your broken mindsets and limiting beliefs. This is the mark of a good mentor. Consultants do not want to offend their clients because they are afraid to lose the profit from the job if the client is not ready to accept what the consultant is teaching. A life coach is not like that; otherwise, he will fail at impacting his clients' lives honestly and powerfully.

When I coach, I always emphasize how my clients cannot buy their inner transformation. As I take on the role of a coach, I commit myself to being authentic and honest with them so they will experience true growth. The ultimate goal is to guide them safely towards their self-set goals.

At times, there's no other way to develop character and commitment to your life performance than undergoing showdowns and overcoming them. Life guides help their clients get through these tough times with encouragement, reminding them to unwrap every gift that comes their way, no matter what the wrapping. Life guides say, "You can do this. It may be tough at the moment, but you know you will be better off."

You Attract What you Focus On

We attract the things we focus on. When you have a mentor, you focus on him and how he lives his life. Therefore, choose a mentor who can close the gap between spirituality and business. People may try to separate these two things from each other, but those who do lack integrity.

How can you become spiritually rich and be financially corrupt? This simply doesn't make sense. You cannot compartmentalize your life. You are either a person of integrity, or you're not. You can be 99.99-percent authentic, but this still doesn't make you a person of integrity.

You have to be 100-percent authentic. A person runs a business based on beliefs, values, and spiritual stances. For those who desperately chase after material wealth, their desperation will eventually lead them to compromise and corruption. That is why they look for people of integrity. Such people are not afraid to speak about their beliefs and what they have experienced in their lives.

All of the mentors I've had overcame showdowns and grew stronger and more successful. Some became bankrupt and regained their wealth. Others faced divorces or health issues and overcame their ordeals.

Amidst it all, there remains one thing in common: they never gave in to becoming victims of circumstance. When choosing a mentor, look for integrity so that you will attract a life of integrity into yourself. Look for someone who does what he says he does, because people of integrity honor their words.

Steps to Having a Life Guide

The first step is to find coaches with integrity who can become your life guides. When with them, watch and listen to them carefully to determine if they're still coping with illusions of their own. The best coaches for you will be those who have overcome your current struggles. If you're going through the same struggles at the same time, how can this coach help you?

The next step is to be ready to pay and perform. Too many people work to accrue material wealth. Successful people work to invest in their own lives so that they can perform better in life. If you are ready to live your life on your terms, it will be a worthy and necessary investment to secure your own life guide. There's no free lunch in the professional coaching business. But your self-development is priceless.

Athletes pay their coaches, though they're the ones who sweat day and night in training, and who run hard, swim hard, or give their all to whatever physical exercise they need to improve their performances. It's the same concept with a life coach. Invest in yourself with money, time, and energy, because the truth is that you're responsible for yourself.

A life performer is someone who operates on the courts rather than in the stands. Your mentors will help get you from A to B, but you're the one who must make the commitment to take this journey and heed their guidance. Imagine, for a moment, that you are at a soccer game where there are fans, commentators, players, and coaches.

Sports commentators analyze the game, talk about the statistics of the players, and comment on the strategies of the coaches. They talk about the actions that are taking place on the field. The fans cheer or boo for their teams. They talk about the action that's going on from the stands. They all only talk about the action, but they don't actually generate any action.

The soccer players and coaches, however, have a say in the points that are being made on the scoreboard. They're the ones who trained with dedication before the event to make the game happen. They're the ones who invested their resources in order to win.

Be a Contribution

As you work on your performance, begin to improve the performance of other people as well as your own. People who have become successful naturally want to make other people discover the happiness and success they've attained. Each one of us has a different way of contributing to the world.

As long as you're ahead in your journey, you can help others on their own journey. Help them achieve a better life. Even if you don't get an immediate reward, you will find that your efforts are completely worth it in the long run. I firmly believe that all people could and should enjoy life on this planet. But I'm not naïve; there are always two sides to every coin that I know. But why would you choose to focus on the downside rather than the pleasant feelings?

Everyone's master plan is designed in a way that each person contributes to the transformation of the world. The more people who experience emotional freedom, the better the world will become. This reminds me of the late Tom Hansberger, who died during my writing of this book. He was an investment legend, a former partner of Sir John Templeton.

Hansberger's behavior toward me mirrored his kindness and honesty. He was also my dear mentor who impacted my life and business in a lot of ways. His thoughtfulness and kindness, though I often found them difficult to understand, provided clarity along my own path. I always felt close with him—he was a great human being, a positive thinker, and a successful achiever. Thank you, Tom, for all your support, help, and tough love.

MENTOR'S SECTION: SIR JOHN TEMPLETON

Sir John Marks Templeton is a pioneer global investor who founded the Templeton Mutual Funds, and who for three decades, devoted his fortune to his Foundation's work, "The Big Questions" of science, religion, and human purpose. He is a pioneer in both financial investments and philanthropy, wherein I saw the connection of how wanting to be a contribution, rather wanting to get rich, creates in you a space for wealth. According to him, when you perceive your wealth as a tool to help others, then you become richer.

Sir Templeton spent his lifetime encouraging open-mindedness. The motto of his Foundation is, "How little we know, how eager to learn," which manifested in how he did business in the financial market and how he carried out his philanthropic work. Starting his career in Wall Street, he went on to create the world's largest and most successful international investment funds. He was able to sell Templeton Funds in 1992 to the Franklin Group for $440 million.

Queen Elizabeth II knighted Sir Templeton in 1987 for his many philanthropic accomplishments, which includes the endowment of the former Oxford Centre for Management Studies as a full college, Templeton College, at the University of Oxford in 1983.

In 1972, he established the world' largest annual award given to an individual, the £1,000,000 Templeton Prize, which is announced in New York and presented in London. The Prize is intended to recognize exemplary achievement in work related to life's spiritual dimension. The prize money was greater than that of the Nobel Prize. It was Templeton's way of putting forward his belief that the spiritual domain was no less important than any other area of human endeavor. Truly, his progressive ideas on finance, faith, and spirituality made him a notable figure in the field of finance and faith.

"If we become increasingly humble about how little we know, we may be more eager to search."

- Sir John Templeton

MENTOR'S SECTION: TOM HANSBERGER

Thomas Hansberger was a value investor and former business partner to Sir John Templeton. Aside from his successful business, he loved hiking, skiing, and traveling. He was also able to compete in and complete several marathons. Hansberger climbed many mountains, such as Mount Kilimanjaro and the Matterhorn, among others.

Besides his dedication to the Christian Youth, he was also involved in many philanthropic works. Even when health issues came up, he kept a positive and grateful attitude toward life. Hansberger was a professional and dedicated man who believed in integrity and human relationships. It's an understatement to say he lived a very full and joyful life.

Hansberger started out his career as a paperboy for his dad. After graduating from school, he served two years in the Air Force in Morocco. While travelling the world he uncovered hidden investment values and started a highly regarded asset management career at the Templeton organization.

Within a few years, Hansberger became President and CEO of Templeton Worldwide. Soon, he oversaw the corporate offices of Templeton, Galbraith, and Hansberger, Ltd (TGH), along with John Galbraith and Sir Templeton.

I was lucky to get a chance to work with Hansberger and the company he founded, Hansberger Global Investors, Inc. During this time I enjoyed the privilege of experiencing his mentorship and leadership Hansberger was a great role model. Always straightforward, professional, kind, and very positive about life, Hansberger truly left a mark in my life.

"There are no shortcuts to success - Keep the faith"

- Tom Hansberger

Special Chapter
Wealth Without a Job

"You should get paid the most for the things that come easiest to you."

Adam Urbanski

Why are Rich People Wealthy?

Did you know that it would take 218 years for Bill Gates to spend all of his money? That is, it would if he spent $1 million a day. His wealth can only be described as financial abundance. Bill Gates and his kind followed their dreams and purposes in life and were able to systemize their business models by building businesses that could essentially run on their own.

Being a great leader, achieving results, and implementing great sales and marketing strategies are infinitely more important than simply having a great product. Entrepreneurs start with an idea, and then they inspire others to join their team. They sell a story, not a product. Bill Gates then purchased the DOS Format from a programmer. Eventually, he founded his successful software company around it.

The secret to financial abundance is to detach yourself from money and focus on living your master plan. The money will follow those who complete the preparation and training stages, stand still, endure, heal, and prepare them to go forward without looking back.

> **TRANSFORMATION PRINCIPLE 19:**
>
> *The secret to financial abundance is to detach from money and focus on living your master plan.*

Many people tend to get stuck in dead-end jobs because of their attachment to money, or the fear that revolves around the lack of money. Such fear keeps people from setting out to achieve their master plans. Such thoughts and feelings unconsciously set people up to live a blueprint of fear attached to a monetary system that is not for the masses. Identifying oneself with such a system will set one on a cycle of perpetual losing and loss. At the end of this chapter, you will see an illustration explaining the results that will come from a life focused on your purpose rather than on money.

The bottom line is this: if your main focus in life is to make money and get rich, no matter how hard you work you may never get there. You may become financially wealthy, but your attachment to money, and the potential for losing it, will generate fear and negativity. Alongside that, the LOA will recognize and respond to both fear and negativity with unwanted results.

Being Essentially Rich

"Wealth without a job," does not mean laziness. It's about being *essentially* rich by doing the things you love and are passionate about. If you pursue your life's purpose, you will reap a monetary harvest. When you're fulfilling your master plan, your life fuel will keep you going. But your energy will quickly drain if you pursue something other than your life's purpose, and you will face burn out or depression. Being emotionally free is about attracting abundance; emotional turmoil, distress, or insecurities will attract lack.

Real entrepreneurs are fascinated by how they can serve the world and change it. They will starve just to make a difference and contribute to society. The innovation and transformation that Microsoft and Apple brought to present and future generations, for example, is a testament to a change that was once incomprehensible. The joy that you will gain from living a life of purpose and significance is priceless.

Attachment to Money vs. Attachment to Purpose

As a result of building your life script, you will experience abundance in all aspects of your life. People, who detach themselves from money, work for the joy of doing so rather than for wealth. They work to fulfill their master plans and life scripts. Their jobs are not just jobs but their missions in life. To be able to do this, one has to go through an attitude shift.

They must start viewing their money must be as a tool for you to carry out your purpose in life and an instrument for you to succeed in your mission. It's a resource to achieve your master plan. Acquiring money is not the master plan of the abundantly rich; instead they use money to form new ventures and continue to grow.

Poor people don't usually admire financially rich people because they view them as mean or unfair. The poor may feel entitled to riches, rather than being grateful for what they currently have. People with this mindset must view the lives of the financially wealthy difference-makers as role models. Many wealthy people focus on how they can make the world a better place. They are not primarily concerned about their image, but about the significance of their contribution.

> **TRANSFORMATION PRINCIPLE 20:**
>
> **Acquiring money is not the master plan of the abundantly rich; instead they use money to form new ventures and continue to grow.**

Success vs. Mediocrity

Mediocrity is a common way of living because it is the easily learned *comfort zone*. But success follows those who take risk and embrace uncertainty. There are no shortcuts, so make sure you learn to be patient for the harvest.

Your life vision is far too important for you to do things half-heartedly. When you're doing a job you dislike just to earn a living, you will always look for shortcuts to get the job done. That is because the end does not represent you. However, when you are the representative of your life goals and create your legacy, you will be dedicated, focused, and involved in your mission.

This is the difference between being successful and mediocre. The successful are constantly learning as students of life. Once you think you know it all, you will stop learning and growing. When there's no growth, there's no life.

180-Degree Change

Leaving the rat race is, in my view, only possible when you rationally decide to make a bold change. You must be ready to turn your life around 180-degrees. You must decide and commit to a period of transformation and learn to embrace uncertainty.

Simply changing external things is not enough. You don't experience transformation by changing habits or behaviors. You don't experience life change by moving from one job to another. If your purpose is to achieve a higher standard of living without detaching from the materialistic worldview, then you're just moving from one rat race to another.

Your blueprint should come from a Be-Do-Have process, not a Do-Have-Be process. When you operate from a Be-Do-Have process, you need to identify first your being. After that, act according to that true being, and eventually have what you need according to who and what your being is.

Every success in life starts with *being* emotionally liberated. Mastering the inner game of wealth and true happiness is not achieved overnight. That is why I wrote this book; I seek to make it as your guide and personal mentor throughout your own process. In this book, I presented my life experiences to help you make the journey through the process to emotional freedom. As always, the beginning is rocky, but once you start on your journey, the feelings of uncertainty begin to stabilize and lift a lot of unwanted weight from your shoulders.

Whenever you're ready, decide to go. A road trip doesn't begin when you get into your car to go. It begins with your decision to go on the trip, because before you can actually go on a trip, you must decide where you will go. Once you know where you want to go, everything becomes clearer. Without goals, you would never get to your destination because you never really knew where that was, to begin with.

The next step will be to start the journey. In life, this means embracing uncertainty. You don't need to know and plan the details of your way. Just let the journey happen, enjoy the ride, and be amazed by the new experiences and growth. Just make sure to check that your car is okay. (Please go back to the training & preparation section of this book for more information on doing that along your life transformation journey). The decision to take the trip is purely rational so feelings should not be involved. Your transformation will begin to take place the moment you make a decision.

TRANSFORMATION PRINCIPLE 21:

Your transformation will begin to take place the moment you make a decision.

CHANGE FOCUS

From Unhealthy Monetary System Towards Healed & Stable Human Relationships

OLD SYSTEM (Still in Place)
Monetary System is Based on Uncovered Paper Money

NO VALUE

WRONG FOCUS

Subconscious Message:
No value
Paper Money losses buying power
Exists in the rat race to make money

NEW SYSTEM
Based on Self-Confidence & Emotional Freedom

REAL VALUE

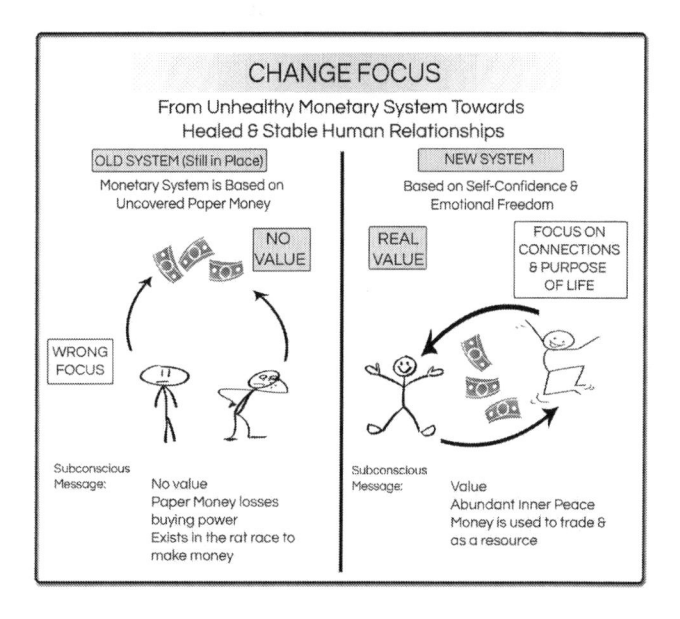

FOCUS ON CONNECTIONS & PURPOSE OF LIFE

Subconscious Message:
Value
Abundant Inner Peace
Money is used to trade & as a resource

Figure 12: Change Focus

You need to shift your focus in life. A lot of people focus on wealth. When you focus on these things, you will experience a lack of significance in life. When you're focused on a sick monetary system, you will experience no value in life. However, once you shift your focus on relationships and your purpose in life, then this is when you'll experience abundant inner peace and emotional freedom. The ability to see money as a tool or as a resource, instead of an end goal, allows you to experience real value in life.

Emotional Freedom is the Key to Financial Freedom

I came to understand that emotional freedom is a prerequisite to having financial abundance. It's impossible to enjoy true financial freedom if one is in emotional bondage under the current unhealthy monetary system. When you notice a change in your emotional level, you can take it as a clear sign of being on track toward acquiring a new view of what real success on a financial level can look like. Be assured that you can never stay in the rat race and become emotionally free.

The Birth of a New Monetary System

Although unhealthy, the monetary system plays a crucial part in a person's life and personal development. It's impossible to be a winner in life unless you become conscious of the insufficiency of money to bring you happiness. It's also impossible unless you begin to focus on what really matters, following your master plan. As long as you're attached to an unhealthy system, you will become unhealthy yourself, often without knowing why.

A person's attachment to a losing system makes them a loser without even knowing it. This may be harsh and difficult to swallow, but if you think about it for a moment, you will understand why I said it. Only detachment from unhealthy feelings and the material could change your life. An emotional detachment will help you set a healthy foundation for life and wealth.

The old system will only change when you start to co-create your life and be the initiator for your healthy internal emotional system. Systems seldom change from outside efforts. Like the old saying goes, change begins within the person himself.

When you experience emotional freedom and help others do the same, then you begin to affect the world. You are able to promote a healthier monetary system, making it accessible to all people rather than an elite few. When you focus on your life's purpose, you are giving birth to a new system within yourself that will be manifested outwardly.

The Phases of a 180-Degree Transformation

Inner transformations work. But be prepared to go through each stage to experience emotional freedom and financial abundance. Buy your Ticket to Life today and enjoy the ride, the challenges of preparation and training, standing still, endurance, healing, and moving forward against the undertow for an amazing new life that you never imagined being possible.

MENTOR'S SECTION: ROBERT KIYOSAKI

Robert Kiyosaki, bestselling author of *Rich Dad, Poor Dad*, is an entrepreneur, investor, motivational speaker, and author. He's also an activist for financial knowledge. In 1969, he graduated from the academy as a deck officer and was honored with the Air Medal after serving in the Vietnam War as a gunship pilot. But in 1975, he left the Marine Corps and worked as a Xerox machine salesperson. He tried several businesses that experienced short-lived success. It was a business that sold Velcro surfer wallets and Heavy metal rock band shirts. In 1997, he established the Cashflow Technologies, Inc.

Kiyosaki then purchased silver mine in South America and took a gold mine public in China. As a teenager, Kiyosaki worked with gold and silver coins. He theorized that with the dollars you have you can buy precious metal coins that will get you ready for the biggest crashes in world history. He opened up my eyes for the illusion of the monetary system.

Kiyosaki is also a real estate investor who spends a lot of his money on big apartment complexes, hotels, and golf courses. He is also the head and investor of oil drilling operations, as well as oil wells, and even a startup solar company. When I look at Kiyosaki's life, I see a man who's going after his master plan. He has a clear life script and he is going for it. This is what makes him truly rich.

> **The rich are those who play to win. The middle class plays not to lose.**
>
> **- Robert Kiyosaki**

Epilogue
The Journey to Angel Mountain (Engelberg), Switzerland

Before setting off for Canada, I had already become intrigued by the idea of mentoring and wanted to take my life in that direction. However, I didn't know whom or what to coach. I wanted to avoid the regular route of coaching. Instead, I wanted to discover my own path and myself so I could guide people by my personal experiences and become a true role model. Any other reason for wanting to be a coach would be unfounded.

When I attended the three-day Millionaire Mind Seminar founded by T. Harv Eker, I was touched at the core. The content of the seminar was practical; it was founded on changing the blueprint and mastering the Inner Game of wealth. It was exactly what I had been looking for.

The combination of spiritual and business growth was a key discovery for finding my own purpose and direction in life. In the same way, you must change yourself inwardly rather than outwardly to change negative behaviors and habits. That was my take-home from the seminar; eventually it served as a turning point in my life.

My journey from Vancouver, Canada to Angel Mountain, Switzerland was led by an inner transformation. It was during that journey that I decided to experiment and test the reality and existence of the LOA. When I left Zurich to go to Canada,

Epilogue

I decided to attain emotional liberation and to discover what financial freedom really meant. I also endeavored to allow the LOA to work in my favor. Every aspect of my life became an experiment that time, and when I let go to test reality, the LOA worked like clockwork.

In the summer of 2005, after a year in Canada, I decided to go back to Switzerland to share what I had learned and experienced. I soon realized that most people could neither understand nor accept my new lifestyle and mindset. However, I began to see the great need for mentoring services that could help my country move forward. I willingly took on the challenge.

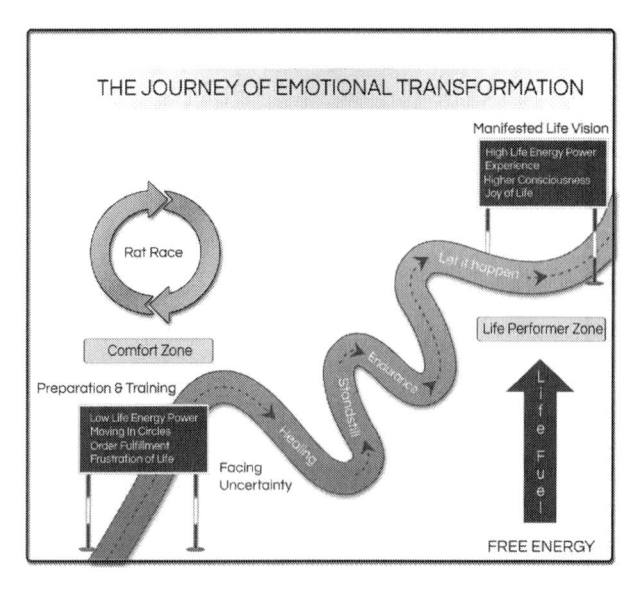

Figure 13: The Journey of Emotional Transformation

In your journey toward emotional freedom, you must go forward courageously and without fear. Have the courage to leave your safe harbor and comfort zone so you can get to a new harbor. Each one of us begins in a state of low life energy; we may have been moving in circles by simply following orders, remaining frustrated in life. However, in your own journey you will reach a state in which you can manifest your life vision and experience the joy of life at the higher level of the consciousness of the Law of Attraction. You will begin from the rat race, but will eventually get from Point A to Point B. Resist the temptation to look for shortcuts. It's important to start with preparation and training, and it's critical that you experience healing, standing still, enduring, and surrendering to let your life vision happen. In your journey, you'll experience a life fuel from the free energy you create from emotional freedom. Leave your comfort zone so that you'll reach your Life Performer Zone.

Preparation and Training

Though my situation at the time was far from how I envisioned for my life, I learned to get by and accepted it as an important period for my growth. I understood the importance of being humble enough to go back to school and get trained. During that preparatory stage in my life, I practiced coaching and process competence techniques, knowing that such preparation was essential to my life's transformation.

Experiencing Process Competence

Back in Switzerland, I sought a new level of consciousness and opened my heart to the possibilities of freedom. The first few weeks of attendance at the S.E.L.F. classes were difficult and bitter. I was used to approaching leadership through professional competence; however, this new system re-educated me to lead and guide by pragmatic approach. The unfamiliarity of the new system sent my mind and all I knew into a tailspin.

In that kind of learning setup, students experienced the practical applications before they developed theories based on the lessons. During that period of education, I learned to differentiate between process and product. Processes are abstracts. In contrast, a process is an awareness of a journey that can be as short as an hour or as long as a lifetime. Eager to begin my new life as a coach and mentor, I sowed my time, energy, and resources so I could enjoy the harvest of my developing life vision one day.

The Fear of Not Making Ends Meet

In my journey from Canada to Switzerland, I closed all doors behind me. Without the option of falling back on old habits, I chose to embrace uncertainty in all its fearful beauty. Returning to Switzerland, I was not as financially strong as I had been a few years prior to leaving for Canada. But emotionally, I was flying high.

My heart was reviving as I began living with purpose rather than simply attempting to make money. I was driven by a goal higher than the desire for financial wealth. I was motivated to experience the fullness of freedom, love, and true success of living by design.

Your decision to escape from the rat race is your declaration that you will no longer be bound by the system. Your decisions from that point should be driven by your life vision. In the rat race, you are concerned with your image and your status in society had likely dictated many of your decisions. You likely found some security in money. But that false sense of safety breeds fear and insecurity, holding people back from living out their true potential and performing at their highest levels.

Building Your Own Life-Entrepreneurial Business for a Profit

I learned to keep the end in sight from the start of any endeavor. What would my life look like in two years? What service could I offer to society? These were some of the questions I asked myself. As I developed a plan and was able to answer them, the fear slowly dissipated. I launched Essential Rich, a coaching company that later became GoLife Life-Entrepreneur Academy.

I started my business with the intent to sell parts of it for a premium to investors who realized its value. When starting a business, always make sure you have an exit strategy. This is not to prepare for failure, but to set up your business correctly so it can operate on a daily basis without you there.

Every business owner invests in his dream in order to reap the harvest at the right time. When your business is strong and capable of running without you, you will be free to live your life outside of the office, doing other things you are passionate about such as travel or charity work. A good business model might sell stakes in your business to investors who will essentially pay you back for the time and money invested in your business. Entrepreneurs often sell company stocks. A prime example is Mark Zuckerberg, CEO of Facebook, who sold a lot of company stocks when Facebook went public, generating massive amounts of wealth and success for himself.

Invest in Yourself

I believe the most common trap that people fall into is to assume their businesses must be profitable from day one. They often overlook the fact that a business requires investment, patience, and nurturing before it can blossom. In the first section of my book, I shared my experiences and the lessons I learned through leaving the rat race behind and making freedom my daily reality.

The process of inner transformation linearly begins with you as an individual. A season of preparation and training must take place before your business and your work performance aligns with your newfound emotional freedom to result in financial freedom. During my journey, I trained myself by reinvesting in education and learning how to market myself in a new way. I sometimes faced the unpleasant necessities of preparation despite the resistance of my Ego against the transformation principles. I decided to become a Life Entrepreneur and Life Guide and to aim at becoming a profitable trader.

Overcoming Old Habits

The Ego will always resist during the preparation and training stages, even as you slowly move into the endurance stage. You will likely be tempted to revert to your old habits. However, as you persevere through the showdowns and shut all doors of the past, new habits will begin to appear.

In my experience, there had been the temptation to go back to the corporate world. But I knew that what I had accomplished and experienced in my pursuit of building my life vision was something I could never trade for a 9-to-5 job and security in paying my next bill. I began to see that my past was an energy-draining way of life. Now I never wanted to allow myself to revisit that stage of my life again.

If investing in your life today means taking out a loan to pay for education, it will be well worth as long as you pay it back when the harvest comes in. Financial debt may be a necessary evil in that early phase. Emotional stability is necessary in such cases, because without it you are at risk of floundering in your faith and inviting more debt and hardship into your life. As you decide to venture into your own journey, clearly identify your own life vision and purpose. Look for ways to serve others and be willing to pay any price that comes with the journey to emotional freedom.

Stand Still, Endure and Heal

This period of my journey taught me the value of delaying gratification both in my finances and my relationships. It brought me from darkness to new life as I learned how to wait for the right time and for things to fall into place, coming to trust that what I had desired to happen would come through practice and patience. Emotional preparation ensured that I came to the journey from a place of inner peace and faith rather than desperation and doubt.

The hardest parts of being patient are maintaining my focus on the present and remaining committed to my vision of the future. It is often far too easy to dwell on the past. But self-control and discipline in the area of waiting yielded a far greater emotional and financial harvest than the temporary satisfaction of giving in to my lesser desires or nostalgia. Therefore, you must let go of distraction and focus on the *not there yet* with gratitude

For me, it meant creating a daily routine and structure that allowed me to focus on the important things at the moment. It also allowed me to focus on what I could accomplish in the here and now. It gave me a road map to ensure that everything I applied myself toward contributed to developing excellence on my way to my life's vision. Therefore, don't forget to pay attention to the details, because they matter. Focus on one day at a time—true-life performance often comes from the details, which many people tend to overlook in favor of massive shifts and changes.

Distance Yourself from Negative People

Your old network of friends and family might not understand the transformative decisions you're making in your life, and that's okay. Now may be the time to create some distance between your life vision and the discouragement around you. Surround yourself with positive people who believe in what you do. As you grow closer to your own purpose, you will likely see the dissipation of old, false relationships. Build a new network of people who want the same things that you do.

Focus on What's Possible Right Now

The transformation period will be difficult because at times you will be tempted to lose faith when you don't see immediate results. This is when patience is a really necessary virtue. With patience, take your focus off of the parts of your life that seem frozen at the moment; instead, think about what you can do in the present.

On my journey to Angel Mountain, I learned to listen to my inner voice and to interpret the signs around me. I practiced visualizing my perfect life in sync with my life's purpose; the clearer I envisioned it to be, the more real it became. My LOA experiment consisted of jotting down the appearance and habits of the woman of my dreams. That very woman finally arrived, but with many life-learning lessons for myself attached. I met her when I least expected--when I learned to be content with myself. She was the woman of my dreams.

In creating your life's script, be sure to include the relationships you desire for yourself. As I wrote down my vision for the perfect mate, I never expected to meet that woman in flesh. She seemed a distant dream. Then suddenly, she was real.

I met her while working hard at my business in a Swiss mountain resort. I quickly realized that I had met her at the right time. Finding her made me learn and grew personally because of my relationship with her after my business associate encouraged me to pursue the woman I called Angel Queen.

This business associate sensed a future between us; he advised me to stay in contact with her. Funny that it was another man's leading that led me to finding the love of my life. But that was the beauty of it. I was given the priceless gift of my dream. No search, no urgency, no online dating. Synchronicity just happened.

Though I knew little about her, I made a bold decision that day and got in touch with her. And the rest is, as they say, history—but didn't end with my bold decision to pursue her. Open your heart without fear of hurt, because the benefits will always outweigh any potential consequences.

When I committed to Angel Queen, I made a decision to go 'all in'. That meant opening my heart to the real possibility of being hurt. But that decision will always be the best I ever made.

In 2009, I visited a professional healer to clear the 'karmic enmeshment' in myself due to a void in my heart. The healer offered me a temporary place to stay, which I gladly accepted as I felt that this could be a key to healing my internal wounds.

I learned so much from her; most importantly, I learned that karmic energies could be very strong—like chains you might not be aware of. Negative karmic energies occur, for example, when a person bears a secret that has kept them following similar patterns in life without even knowing it. I recommend that every reader of this book does some research into karma and energy patterns. Without understanding this key idea, you might attempt hundreds of therapies that will not lead you to inner peace.

Apparently, these therapies cannot break through the patterns. Sometimes karma is sealed by ancient dogmas; similar to decrees we have placed on ourselves. Decrees are like strong belief patterns, which you might not be aware of because they were silently established in the past.

When you experience something in yourself that you cannot change, look deeply at your roots, where you are coming from, and where you are today. Sometimes, it comes in the form of illness. Families may have had generation after generation in which a member of their family died from the same disease. In other situations, generations of families may have suffered from an unfaithful spouse committing adultery. Generation after generation, they witness the same thing. This is the pattern of karmic enmeshment.

My "First Time" at Angel Mountain

The healer helped me clean out my own karmic enmeshments. I became aware of what was behind the curtains, so I was able to effectively clear myself. As I learned and closed the door on the cycles that were a part of my life, I discovered more about my own history and origins.

The way I came about that discovery can only be described as serendipitous. As I sat at dinner one night with Angel Queen, I learned that she was originally from Angel Mountain. I had heard of that place, but I had never experienced going there.

My mother later told me her own story, which turned out to be the story of me. She worked as a hotel receptionist at Angel Mountain, a beautiful mountain resort in central Switzerland. That was the place where my own began at conception.

I could hardly believe what I'd heard, but it all made sense, providing the clarity and closure I needed for the negative patterns in my life. It also gave me confidence to follow the signs I was seeing and the connections I was making. With Angel Queen at my side and my history revealed, I decided to go to Angel Mountain, back to my roots and to the chance to restart my life.

When the door opened and all signs pointed that way, I took the leap without hesitating. My Ego had never been removed whenever I made a decision. Though not intentionally looking for signs, they had all fallen into place. Angel Queen. Angel Mountain. Myself.

I allowed myself to be patient in the discovery period. I then took the risk of moving my life to a new place, uncertain of the outcome. I whisked my life up to the heavenly place of Angel Mountain, which I am still pleased to call my home today.

My Piece of Heaven on Earth

Circumstances brought me here, but I knew that the LOA was strongly in motion. Angel Mountain is described as Switzerland's summer and winter holiday paradise. It is a tourist-friendly village visited by people from around the world. It is graced with a view of the Benedictine Monastery; it is a wonderful, unspoiled countryside against an impressive mountain backdrop.

It has a modern and extensive cable car system that takes you to all directions, including the top of Mount Titlis, which is 3,239 m (10,627 ft.). Great restaurants, cozy mountain huts, and accommodations adorn the resort. When I got there, I felt protected and completely well. I found an irreplaceable treasure by opening and following my heart.

Finding a Home in Angel Mountain

Part of my master plan is to live in a place that feels like perpetual vacation. When I arrived in Angel Mountain, I did not know where I was going to live. I contacted several realtors, but they were unable to help me; they only sold homes. But one realtor went out of his way to show me a place that was for rent.

With my firm belief against coincidences, I knew that this was meant to be. After all, I had declared early on that I wanted to live in a place like that. It felt like I was on holiday and I found myself in a complete tourist destination. Everything was falling into place.

When you let go of emotional and financial burdens, you will be free and open to all of life's possibilities. I knew that whatever I had built into my master plan would be taken care of regardless of my financial situation. The whole experience gave me the humility to ask for what I wanted and to accept a "No" response. After all, a "No" is just a "No"; it won't really define you.

I opened up an inner room for my desires. In my old life, I was faced with so many limitations, which I allowed to persist. I had given up on certain dreams because I thought they were crazy or impossible. But as I grasped this new emotional freedom, I realized that in *my* movie script, *I* decide what's possible and what's not.

Waiting for Angel Queen

The keys to true success are patience in focusing on what matters day to day, and keeping the purpose of life in mind. I often ask myself: What would my feelings be if…? This question released a lot of stress and made me feel less weighed-down day-to-day, even while tangible results were still missing. My Angel Queen was an inspiration in so many ways as I learned and grew in patience and gratitude.

We were brought together for a purpose, even if I was unaware that our first meeting would lead us both to our future. There are always a process to follow and timing in life that cannot be overridden. For Angel Queen, the timing was not right. She wasn't ready for a commitment, so I went back to the waiting room.

There, I had the option of desperation or focusing on projects in my life that I *was* able to accomplish. With the encouragement and kindness of those around me, I chose the second option. I painstakingly learned that one cannot force the future into the present; you have only to keep the faith, and clean out your closest of old karmic energies and the LOA will prevail.

Fears will creep up when you least expect them trying to keep you from making decisions that will take you outside of the comfort zone. But the emotional conflicts that come when you take steps into the unknown are the beginning stages of healing the old wounds of the past. Once you are healed, the pain will be gone forever. After you experience standstill, endurance and healing, forever means forever.

I've had my fair share of turbulent relationships when my family became estranged with me because of what they perceived as strange changes in my life. But things eventually fell into place. Today, I enjoy a loving relationship with myself, the effects of which are sent out to others through the LOA. It is clear that it is all about your own transformation while healing, loving, and caring about yourself

Confrontations are important because breakthroughs come through questioning the status quo. After enduring conflicts, you will be stronger, happier, and most importantly, loving.

Love is the strongest energy available that cannot be explained in words. Love just is. The journey to emotional and financial freedom will guide you in the process toward love because it's not just a simple overnight switch or a quick fix. You cannot control if some members of your family accept or reject you because of your decisions to leave the status quo, but you *can* decide to keep your faith and open your heart without fear of getting hurt.

Taking a position and stance for your own life vision takes courage. Despite the resistance I've encountered, I endured. As a result, I reconciled with my family *and* got to enjoy emotional security and love. This is my deepest wish for all of you. So face whatever conflicts and issues have been left buried in your heart and your family, so that you can let Love happen to you.

"If someone is not treating you with love and respect, it is a gift if they walk away from you. If that person doesn't walk away, you will surely endure many years of suffering with him or her. Walking away may hurt for a while, but your heart will eventually heal. Then you can choose what you really want. You will find that you don't need to trust others as much as you need to trust yourself to make the right choices."

— Miguel Ruiz, *The Four Agreements: A Practical Guide to Personal Freedom*

Moving Forward without Looking Back

There will always be room for learning and growth in life, but there is only one transformation from caterpillar to butterfly. Once you are transformed, you will never go back to your old ways. Now you are in performance and fun mode. You are flying high and getting to observe the world in a different attitude from a new altitude. But flying can be dangerous if you are careless, so focus on living responsibly and focusing on your life script:

The Four Agreements according to Miguel Ruiz:

1. 1. Be impeccable with your word
2. 2. Don't take anything personally
3. 3. Don't make assumptions
4. 4. Always do your best

— Miguel Ruiz, The Four Agreements: A Practical Guide to Personal Freedom

Always do your best. Because anything worth doing is worth doing well, be as professional as you can be. So, through this book, I hope to give the readers the best reading and learning experience possible even if I will never fully reach their expectations. When you pursue your life calling, give it your best. You are only as good as your last work.

The Power of Meditation

Meditation clears the mind from constant chatter and helps you to focus your thinking upward toward your life purpose and master plan. But meditation alone will not move you closer to manifesting your goals. I have seen people in their somewhat financially secure comfort zones meditate in every way they can. That's okay as long it happens in the preparation and training period. But people cannot stay indefinitely in the mediation stage; they have to move into action and living. Find your own way of meditating and make it routine, then you will do it without effort and have time in your life to live.

Meditation clears the mind from thought; it's within the stillness that follows that you can reconnect with your higher self or what is commonly called intuition. The clarity of intuition and the fearlessness with which you step toward it are open line to receiving whatever you have asked for.

When I began my quest for a new company logo, my intuition told me to make a money tree the icon of my business. At that time, I had never heard of a money tree, so was quite pleased when I learned the significance of it in Chinese legend. The money tree is a holy tree that brings fortune and luck; it is a symbol of nobility and affluence. The coins of the tree connect paradise with the material bounty of the world.

Meditation also helps you to focus on building your life script and to come to a point in which your clarity and intuition can freely flow in emotional freedom. Different methods work for different people. It's completely subjective. Some do yoga while others immerse themselves in nature. Others will find time to read the Bible.

The important thing for you to do is to make time to meditate on a daily basis because it's so easy to get caught up in the day-to-day business of life and forget about what matters. When you don't give yourself time to refresh your mind and heart, you'll end up increasing the clutter on the inside. Meditation clears the clutter and renews peace, allowing you to keep you mental focus on the big vision and master plan.

The Combination that Leads to Harvest

As you navigate through your new course you will be able to enjoy a winning combination of improved feelings and intuition converted into real life results. Be prepared to receive the harvest of your planting and tending; through mediation, resistance will finally dissolve.

Opening your heart and reestablishing its connection with the world will enable to express your real feelings without fears of rejection. In addition, your encounters with others will finally align with your life's purpose. Once you recognize and humbly admit to the role of a higher power in your life, allow life to take you on a journey of peace and gratitude. In this journey, you will meet unpleasant or sharp turns at times, but such moments will help you arrive at your life vision. Just remember to magnify the possibilities and limit the weaknesses and negativity.

All that you've read in this book is the true story of a man who was lucky enough to be pushed past his comfortable limits to realize his own power as a co-creator of his life. The science of the transformational process of the journey brought him to a better place, even when the mountains, the sea and the land appeared the same as before. Through this journey of healing, feeling, and finding his roots, he found the true purpose of life. *I* am that man.

This new life was my dream come true. I had always known somewhere deep inside that the dream existed. However, it seemed so distant from me and from all that I knew. The power of faith will always win out, even when you cannot see yourself arriving anytime soon at your destination—you will get there. Learn, grow, and repeat every day. You can never be satisfied to arrive at a single destination. Enjoy and keep growing and performing.

Keep dreaming big.

Only then can big things happen in reality.

Erich Perroulaz

Bibliography

"Astronaut Bio: Edgar Dean Mitchell." (2007). Retrieved online on November 7, 2014 at http://www.jsc.nasa.gov/Bios/htmlbios/mitchell-ed.html

Batchelor, D. (n.d.s). "Who is Michael The Archangel?" Retrieved online on September 22, 2014 at http://www.amazingfacts.org/media-library/book/e/85/t/who-is-michael-the-archangel.aspx

Barker, C. & Holmes, E. (1953). *365 days of richer living*. USA: Science of Mind Publishing.

"Biography: Sir John Templeton." (n.d.). Retrieved online on September 22, 2014 at http://www.sirjohntempleton.org/biography.asp

"Dr. Judith Orloff's biography." (n.d.). Retrieved online on November 7, 2014 at http://www.drjudithorloff.com/about-judith-orloff.htm

Earle, M. & Rogin, N. (1980). "The context for creating a transformed world: a world that works for everyone." Retrieved from http://wernererhardbiography.com/a-shot-heard-round-the-world/

Erhard, W. and Gioscia, V. (1975, May). The Est standard training. *Journal of Individual Psychology, (31) 1*.

Erhard, W. Guerin, G. & Shaw, R. (1975). "The mind's dedication to survival." *Journal of Individual Psychology, 31*(1).

Erhard, W., Jensen, M., Zaffron, S., Granger, K., Echeverria, J. (2013). Being a leader and the effective exercise of leadership: An ontological/phenomenological model. Harvard Business School Negotiation, Organizations and Markets Research Papers.

Flandro, C. (2011). "The legacy of Elizabeth Clare Prophet." Retrieved online on September 22, 2014 at http://www.bozemandailychronicle.com/100/newsmakers/article_03a800bc-d139-11e0-ab6a-001cc4c03286.html

Goddard, N. (1977). *Immortal man*. Camarillo, CA: DeVorss & Company.

Hanley, J. P. (1989). *Lifespring - getting yourself from where you are to where you want to be*. New York: Simon & Schuster.

Heidegger, M. (2010). *Being and time*. New York: State University of New York Press.

Holliwell, R. (1992). *Working With The Law*. Phoenix, Arizona: Church and School of Christian Philosophy.

Howell, E. (2013). "Edgar Mitchell: sixth man on the moon." Retrieved online on November 7, 2014 at http://www.space.com/20393-edgar-mitchell-biography.html

"Jordan Belfort biography." (n.d.). Retrieved online on November 7, 2014 at http://www.biography.com/people/jordan-belfort-21329985#synopsis

"Joseph Murphy." (n.d.). Retrieved online on September 22, 2014 at http://emmetfox.net/Joseph%20Murphy%20Page.htm

Krisco, K. H. (1997). *Leadership and the art of conversation*. Prima Publishing.

Martin, E. (2014). It Would Take Bill Gates 218 Years To Spend All His Money. Retrieved from, http://www.businessinsider.com/years-for-bill-gates-to-spend-his-fortune-2014-10

Mountrose, P. & Mountrose, J. (NA). "Biography of Wallace Wattles, author of The Science of Getting Rich." Retrieved online on September 22, 2014 at http://gettingthru.org/science-getting-rich/science-of-getting-rich-articles/wallace-wattles-biography/

Murphy, J. (2010). *The power of your subconscious mind.* Princeton, New Jersey: The Princeton Licensing Group.

Oster, K. (2013). "Entrepreneurs & dreamers: Marie Forleo, the manifesting magician." Retrieved online on November 7, 2014 at http://www.rebellesociety.com/2013/01/21/entrepreneurs-dreamers-marie-forleo-the-manifesting-magician/

"Paulo Coelho." (n.d.). Retrieved online on September 22, 2014 at http://www.famousauthors.org/paulo-coelho

Price, J.R. (1997). *The Spiritual Philosophy for the New Word.* Carlsbad, California: Hayhouse

"Rhonda Byrne." (n.d.). Retrieved online on September 22, 2014 at http://www.famousauthors.org/rhonda-byrne

"Robert Kiyosaki." (n.d.). Retrieved online on September 22, 2014 at http://www.famous-entrepreneurs.com/robert-kiyosaki

Smothermon, R. (1980). *Winning through enlightenment.* San Francisco: Context Publication.

Sommer, C. (2012). "When you've got it – flaunt it: A case study on Marie Forleo." Retrieved online on November 7, 2014 at http://www.forbes.com/sites/carisommer/2012/02/22/when-youve-got-it-flaunt-it-a-case-study-on-marie-forleo/

"Steven Spielberg biography." (n.d.) Retrieved online on November 7, 2014 at http://www.biography.com/people/steven-spielberg-9490621#synopsis

Zaffron, S. & Logan, D. (2009). *The three laws of performance.* Jossey-Bass.

Ticket To Life is a brand of Essential Rich

Do what you love and make money out of it!

To learn more, visit Ticket To Life International by going to www.lifeticket.net.

If you want to contact us, you may email support@lifeticket.net.

If you want to connect with us for VIP coaching and corporate workshops, please email sales@lifeticket.net.

You may also reach us at the following phone numbers:

Within United States: +1(914)987-6934

Outside of the United States: +883 510-001-287-5711

An Invitation to Come Visit Angelmountain (Engelberg)

Angelmountain (Engelberg) became my home. The fact that it's called "Angelmountain" is apt for how it became my piece of heaven on earth. It is where I found my roots and began to live a renewed life.

Located in the heart of Switzerland, you should definitely make your way down to this place because of the panoramic views of the mountain scenery. There are a lot of things you can do at Angelmountain that makes it the perfect holiday destination. This place has one of the longest ski slopes in Switzerland with a 2000-meter descent from Titlis to Engelberg. It also has the highest suspension bridge, the Titlis Cliff Walk, if you're after an adrenaline rush. The cozy hotels, holiday apartments, restaurants, and bars will make sure you'll have a relaxing holiday.

I found my home here. Maybe, you too will find something special in this little heaven on earth.

ENGELBERG
TITLIS

http://www.engelberg.ch/en/

Acknowledgements

Writing a book can be a lonesome business. It initially appears to be an individual task. However, this book is not just a writing process as it comes together with many parts already somewhere stored in a file or in the heart.

My thanks and deep gratitude goes out to all the people who let me grow and finds my way—on purpose or not.

Special thanks go to my family, friends and colleagues for their patience, care and help all throughout the years when I was not aware of emotional freedom and self-love, when I was looking for external factors to make me happy. Truly, it's never easy to get along with somebody who is looking to find his roots and his own way.

Thank you to all of you who let me go and gave me chances to do better.

Thank you to my family and Angel Queen.

I would like to extend my deepest gratitude to the following people who have taken part in turning this book from a vision into a powerful reality:

A special thanks goes to Kim Dy and the *Innovation Solutions* Team (kim@innovatingsolutions.net; www.innovatingsolutions.net), my personal writing coach for the dedication, professional attitude and patience in manifesting this book.

Acknowledgements

Vetta Bogdanoff (vetta.bogdanoff@gmail.com), for proofreading and editing

Haresh R. Makwana, (hrmjrio2011@gmail.com), Thank you very much Haresh for the stylish and beautiful book cover design.

Benz Websolutions, for the Website Design.

Made in the USA
Middletown, DE
14 November 2018